Putting Improv to W

Putting Improv to Work

Spontaneous Performance
for Professional and Personal Life

GREG HOHN

Toplight

Jefferson, North Carolina

ISBN (print) 978-1-4766-8775-9 ∞
ISBN (ebook) 978-1-4766-4635-0

LIBRARY OF CONGRESS AND BRITISH LIBRARY
CATALOGUING DATA ARE AVAILABLE

Front cover image © 2022 ProStockStudio/Arta Karya/Shutterstock

Printed in the United States of America

Toplight is an imprint of McFarland & Company, Inc., Publishers

*Box 611, Jefferson, North Carolina 28640
www.toplightbooks.com*

To my parents, Elaine and John,
for instilling in me both artistry and practicality,
and to Transactors Improv Company and Jim Dean
for the opportunities they've given me.

Acknowledgments

Thank you to my proofreader, researcher, staunchest supporter, wisest counsel, greatest source of laughs, and wife, April. I am also grateful to the individual members of Transactors Improv over the years; you have taught and inspired me, and I can't imagine what my life would have been like without you in it. Thanks to the faculty, administration, and staff at UNC Kenan-Flagler Business School for work that is both meaningful and fun and especially to my area chairpersons, Heidi Schultz and Judy Tisdale who have always had my back and been open to my ideas. I'm deeply grateful to Toplight Books for their interest in publishing this book. Jaybird O'Berski has been an enthusiastic and steadfast supporter and source of advice. Ellen Hemphill has been an artistic mother to me. Mimi Herman and John Yewell have been literary muses and sources of commiseration and encouragement. Carl Schutts, you exposed me to improv back in 1977 at Minneapolis Central High School and got me hooked. And, finally, to my students at UNC, Duke, and elsewhere, you have taught me as much as I have taught you, and this book wouldn't exist without you.

Table of Contents

Preface

This book outlines a very successful applied improv course I've taught to MBA candidates since 2000. It's arranged sequentially with the activities described, for both groups and individuals, generally building on each other. The plan evolved out of improv courses I taught for stage performers.

You don't have to be an MBA student to understand or benefit from this book. You don't have to be a student, technically speaking, at all. Throughout the book I've used "participant," "player," and "student" interchangeably, and you can substitute "colleague," "subordinate," "people," "comrade," "peon," or whatever suits your needs. Regardless of the terminology, I hope that all sorts of professionals (I've worked with a very wide range of them) can benefit from the book.

I also hope that educators, including trainers and facilitators, can adapt it for teaching, designing, and even proposing their own courses, regardless of subject. I've assigned many of the chapters as class reading, so it could serve as a textbook. Perhaps the book will be helpful for directors and actors in theater, scripted and unscripted, as well as other artists. (I've worked with a lot of them too.)

So what is improv? For the purposes of this book, improv— short for "improvisation"—is spontaneous, unscripted performance. My specialty and background are in live improv onstage. But improv applies to all sorts of art forms, including obvious ones like music and dance and not-so-obvious ones like painting and cooking. Improv also shows up in all manner of sports, both team and individual.

And we improvise in our everyday lives, in professional, social, organizational, academic, personal, and other settings. We might have desires and plans in these situations, but we generally have to react to the people and circumstances around us and adapt to them to be successful. This is applied improv, putting the principles and techniques of unscripted theater to use in nontheatrical settings.

What is improv not?

Improv is definitely not stand-up comedy, which is almost always tightly scripted. Indeed, improv doesn't have to be comedic at all. This book won't teach you to be funny—although you might find yourself discovering and getting comfortable with your native sense of humor as opposed to merely repeating others' jokes. Moreover, there's just about nothing less funny than someone *trying* to be funny, regardless of the setting, so let's set humor aside for now.

Improv is also not amateurishly winging it. At least good improv isn't. A good improviser practices technique and prepares for situations. A good improviser responds to the reality of evolving scenarios rather than forcing a plan. A good improviser is aware of and responsive to both internal and external stimuli. These practices are as valuable in real life as they are on a theater stage.

My improv experience is extensive. I started performing improvisational theater professionally in 1989 when I joined Transactors Improv in Chapel Hill, North Carolina, and began teaching it shortly afterward. In 1996 I became director of Transactors.

In the late '90s I began developing my applied improv curriculum, and in 2000 I started teaching it as a full-term, for-credit course at the University of North Carolina's Kenan-Flagler Business School. I became a full-time faculty member at UNC Kenan-Flagler in 2012 and have the rank of clinical assistant professor. I also taught in Duke University's Theater Studies Department for five years and have led applied improv sessions in a wide array of settings across the USA and occasionally outside of it.

In this book I draw upon and refer to my background as a teacher, director, and performer and in other roles as well. I'd like to emphasize that the activities I describe were invented by other people. Even activities I thought I made up were, it turns out, originated by others; I just didn't know about it. I can claim original interpretations and applications of improv activities, but even there I've been influenced by others. No one is an island.

My teachers have been many. Some of them you might have heard of and some not. Many haven't even been stage improvisers. If you want names, okay. I studied pretty extensively with Paul Sills and

Mick Napier and have had shorter learning experiences with Joe Bill, Del Close, Michael Gellman, Susan Messing, Mark Sutton, and others. I've lifted (and changed) ideas I got from them—but then they probably borrowed them from someone else. One game, for instance, I learned from Paul Sills, who probably learned it from his mother, Viola Spolin, who probably learned it from Neva Boyd, who probably observed children playing it as they have for millennia.

I'm grateful to all my teachers, as well as my colleagues and students, for all they've taught me, and I don't wish to slight anyone. However, there's no way I can accurately trace who taught me what. My goal isn't to tell the history of improv and its exercises and games. There are other, better sources for that, and I've listed some of them elsewhere in this book.

While I've been teaching in higher education for decades, this is not a classically academic book. Similarly, this is not a scientific book even though I've tried to support my assertions with scientific evidence. Studies often mention the significance of the placebo effect, and I'm a big believer in it, but I hope to offer more than just that. Ultimately, I don't want you to believe in me as much as I want you to use my techniques as a way to believe in yourself.

So welcome aboard the improv train. In addition to being the engineer and telling you about my experiences, thoughts, and feelings, I'll also give you a chance to drive your own train, both solo and with others. Choo choo!

Learning Versus Teaching: Some Notes for Students and Teachers

Before we leave the station (and this tiresome train metaphor), I'd like to say a few things about my approach to teaching. I much prefer dialogue to lecture, even to the extent that I've occasionally been flummoxed when asked to speak to a group and not also to listen to it.

I don't like to tell people what they'll learn or what they just learned. Rather I prefer that participants tell each other and me what they learned. I'm not trying to shirk my responsibility as a teacher or come across as some mysterious Zen master in saying this. Some students get one thing out of an exercise, and others get something totally different or nothing at all. Once I start saying that there are things you're *supposed* to learn from an exercise, your mind might be focused on what you think *I* think is important rather than what *you* think is important. I love it when people see perspectives and angles that I might have missed.

Improv is exploration, and exploration requires patience and an open mind. Exploring is different from commuting. On your daily trip to work or school or wherever, you know where you're going, and your goal is generally to get there as quickly as possible. Exploration, on the other hand, goes wherever it goes. The goal is to be in the process as opposed to ending the process, as is the case with commuting. You might have a goal of finding something specific, but true exploration is open to finding anything or even nothing.

Exploration can be challenging for groups as well as individuals. What a group gets out of an applied improv event depends on what the focus of the program is and what happens during that program. An applied-improv communication workshop will likely result in a stronger esprit de corps among participants. Likewise, a team-building program should also improve team members' communication. It's a winning situation as long as the participants are open to the results.

Improv is very subjective and probably impossible to quantify, but one great thing about it is that you can jump right in. If you want to play the violin, for example, you'll need to practice for months or years to gain any sort of competency. Improv, on the other hand, merely requires skills we regularly use. If you can communicate, that's about all it takes to get started. That's not to say you won't struggle, but the struggle is mostly about what's going on in your head. What do you perceive? How do you react? What do you think? What do you do and say?

Improv is about action, and no amount of reading or cogitating is a substitute for that. To that end I hope you'll engage in this book's activities. Improv also requires commitment. You must steep yourself in the experience before you can reflect on it later.

Thus, when giving instructions for an activity, I'll answer questions about how to do it and often remind participants to be aware of what they're experiencing, observing, thinking, and feeling while doing it. However, I avoid answering "why" questions, promising instead that we'll address them after the activity.

By focusing on anything other than the activity itself, we might miss the meaning of what we're doing. Sometimes the meaning of an experience is simply committing to it. Or, as Paul Sills used to exhort his students, often spiritedly and spiced liberally with f-bombs, "Do the thing. Play the game!"

During the COVID pandemic, I was forced to teach applied improv online, something I thought was impossible until I did it—with the help and encouragement of students and administrators. In describing the activities I use, I have tried to mention adaptations and alternatives for virtual environments. These might also be useful if members of your in-person group have mobility issues or differing physical abilities. Improv is all about adaptation, and thus I believe we can include everyone.

Improvisation is just another way of saying "not knowing." You don't know what's going to happen in improv because it hasn't happened yet. This is scary because most people, including this writer, are afraid of the unknown. Most of us also want to know what the rules are. We want to know how we can gauge our success or failure. This is how we're schooled; someone tells us what we're learning. Once we're out of school though, we have to figure out so much for ourselves. No teacher is waiting to reveal the answer if we can't find it on our own.

What's more, most of us are afraid we're going to screw up something. But how can you screw up if the boundaries of right and wrong haven't been set? Looking at it from a theatrical perspective, if you're reciting one of Cordelia's speeches from *King Lear*, you might well be afraid of blowing the lines you're supposed to say, which were written by a master and have been spoken for centuries. But what if the script stated: "Cordelia: [*Says whatever she says*]?" Well, for some of us that's scarier because it's so ambiguous.

Navigating ambiguity—and looking at it as opportunity rather than hazard—is a key to successful improvisation on or offstage. Improv allows us to go beyond certainty without freaking out, to get comfortable with ambiguity and even flourish in it.

"Be prepared" is the Scouts' motto, and that organization does a good job of giving kids the means, chiefly through sets of skills, to respond to many different situations. The Scouts are not taught to bring every possible tool they might need. Rather they are taught to improvise adaptations using a few rudimentary tools and knowledge. A Scout can thus do things like dig the Erie Canal with a spork or perform arthroscopic surgery using nothing but a flashlight and a length of string. Or so I'm told. The Scouts are empowered to adapt.

My goal as an educator and author is to do the same thing. I want to give my students and readers a set of virtual tools and let them determine how to use them. People get different lessons and applications from the same activity or discussion. A status exercise might benefit someone in sales differently from how it benefits someone in HR. Someone else might apply what they learned at home or in a social or athletic setting. I usually avoid specific applications because I'm not a specialist in the areas my students are. However, I'm eager to learn about specific takeaways, particularly if my students are sharing specialized knowledge with each other.

Be patient as you embark on your applied improv journey. It's improv, and you're not supposed to know where you're going. Enjoy the ride. Recognize that the experience differs from person to person. Understand that you might not "get" an activity at first and maybe not ever. You'll have to think about what you might have learned and how to use it instead of being told what you were taught. The most important thing is that you have the experience and examine it.

And have some fun too.

Most young animals play, and I'm talking about animals like lions and dogs here, not necessarily cockroaches and herring. Observe their play, and you can see its application to their adult lives. Maybe their frolicking is similar to hunting, fighting, or flight. It's not serious now, but it eventually could become that way. The play of children can be seen in the same way. Their play is not only fun and recreational, but it's also practice for future serious situations.[1]

If you as an adult, and maybe a very important adult at that, can look at play as practice in a safe environment, then you might well be more inclined to explore it. Play provides an opportunity to explore risk and to learn in a situation where the stakes are low or nonexistent. So, if you're worried about looking foolish playing a silly game and risking nothing, I wonder how you'll handle serious situations when the stakes are high.

Maybe you can even get into the frame of mind one of my successful former MBA students wrote me about. In a client meeting one day he realized that instead of seeing the person he was doing business with as an adversary, he was seeing a partner. "We were *playing* business."

Introduction

Beware the Refrigerator in the Road

One of my brothers had a friend, John, who bought a car one day. When my brother asked him what brand it was, John replied, "Um, it's a ... a Pedros." It turns out it was a Peugeot. Not remembering what kind of car he bought wasn't the biggest head-scratcher John ever did though.

No, that might have been totaling his Pedros. One night he was driving on a highway when he saw a refrigerator in his lane. He drove right into it. Asked why he didn't avoid the appliance, John reasoned, "Why would there be a refrigerator on the freeway?" Lest I be accused of judging John too harshly, I should add that, based on my experiences in the classroom and theater, I think many of us would plow into a fridge if it were in our way.

In a play I saw an actor drop a glass, which crashed on the floor. Everyone in the audience saw and heard it happen. The actors certainly did—hell, they were standing in it! But neither actor responded to the broken glass because it wasn't in the script, although it was undeniably happening.

People drop glasses fairly frequently in real life, and the actors could have just picked up the glass and continued with their lines. The vast majority of the audience wouldn't have even known that dropping the glass wasn't in the script. By not responding to the accident the actors demonstrated that they weren't in the moment of the play and drew attention to the original mistake.

Now, in improv we're looking and hoping for that dropped glass (even though we don't use real glasses) because the best improvised scenes seem to happen by accident. That "accident" would be something that's actually occurring onstage, set within a context, and not just an idea that one of the players is trying to bring to life. So good improvisers strive to be aware of and to respond to everything that happens onstage.

The worst improv scenes often involve players totally missing what's happening onstage. Ideas and expectations can blind actors to organic developments. Opportunities, some of which are obvious to the audience, are ignored as players try to impose their will upon a scene. Missing these offers, these accidents, indicates that an improviser is in their head rather than present in the scene and moment.

Actors in scripted works can also be guilty of being in their heads and not in the moment, even when they're not dropping glasses or other props. I've seen actors respond to lines that haven't been said yet. That suggests that the actor is still on the page in the book rather than onstage in the moment and also forces their scene partners out of the moment.

In nontheatrical situations there's a danger to "not seeing the refrigerator" aside from actually running into refrigerators. I've seen presenters so wed to their plans that they can't adapt to what's happening around them. This can be as simple as not repeating a word or phrase when a loud noise such as a sneeze overpowers the speech. Or it can take the form of responding to a question with a "canned" answer that winds up being irrelevant or even inappropriate.

In my courses and described later in this book is an exercise called Mockery of a Mock Interview. We send an interviewee out of the room and have them return to face an interviewer to whom we have given disturbing or distracting behaviors. Often the interviewees fail to respond to the interviewer and what's happening. Rather than adapting to the moment, these interviewees plow ahead with what they've rehearsed even if it seems not to be working.

However, there are those interviewees who *will* respond to what's actually happening. If the interviewer keeps looking at their watch, the interviewee might say something like, "I see you're checking the time. Would another time be better for us to meet?" How cool! By being in the moment you can respond to it assertively and adapt to it. You won't *control* what's occurring but at least you're not a helpless victim of circumstance.

When we discuss this exercise in class, students share horror stories from real-life interviews, ranging from interviewers' deliberate monopolization of conversations to their turning out the lights and leaving interviewees in the dark! These stories suggest to me that interviewers are more interested in how aware and responsive potential employees are than in the prospects' backgrounds, which interviewers already know from résumés.

"Look where you want to go" is a motorcycling maxim that's saved my bacon many times. I think it also applies to everyday life and theater. If you're paying attention to what's happening right now, you can respond to it, just as you would to the curves in a road. If you go straight when the road curves, you're probably not heading for a good outcome. And if you're staring at the ditch, afraid you're going to wipe out, instead of looking where the road goes and trying to follow it, you'll probably wind up in that ditch.

"See what you see, not what you think you see," improv guru Paul Sills used to say, and I imagine he'd also apply that to what you think you *don't* see. Dwight Eisenhower, who was not an improv guru but rather a general and president, said, "Plans are useless, but planning is everything." Plan to be surprised. Prepare for your plans to be obsolete. Be ready to adapt.

It's like those road signs that warn, "Be prepared to stop." Shouldn't we *always* be prepared to stop? After all, there might be a refrigerator in the road.

1

Self-Consciousness and the Spotlight Effect

"[Y]ou will never make a good impression on other people until you stop thinking about what sort of impression you're making..."—C.S. Lewis

Self-interest is human nature. That can be good in that it motivates self-preservation. It can also be bad in that it often leads to selfishness and solipsism. Either way, self-interest casts us in the starring role of our life story, and that makes sense because we experience existence through the lens of our selves. At its extreme, self-interest can make us believe that we're the center of everyone's attention and not just our own. Psychologists call this the spotlight effect.[2]

The spotlight effect can take us out of the moment and into our heads because we're worried that other people are watching our every move, noticing our every mistake, and judging us. This self-consciousness can consume a lot of mental and emotional energy, energy we need if we're going to improvise well, onstage or off it. The louder the voices get in our head, the harder it is to hear, see, and react to what's going on outside it.

The fallacy at the heart of the spotlight effect is pretty obvious once you think about it. If everyone is focusing on themselves, then how can they simultaneously focus on us?

Moreover, the judgment we imagine others passing on us is usually negative but can also be grandiosely positive. Either way, what we imagine is probably not accurate and therefore not worthwhile. The judging we feel is likely more an indication of how we feel about ourselves. We know what we're trying to do, how we're not doing it right, how we always do this or that. In other words, we have both an insider's view of and emotional baggage about ourselves that others do not and largely cannot have.

Even in situations where others *are* actively judging and evaluating us, such as interviews, presentations, auditions, and client meetings, they're not judging us the way we're judging ourselves. Our audiences usually don't know what we're going to say, at least not nearly as well as we do. The audience doesn't know when we've forgotten something or said it worse than we expected we would—unless we tell them (which is something we'll cover later).

Our audience isn't as familiar with us as we are with ourselves. And we all know familiarity breeds contempt, right? It seems to me that most people, including me, are much harsher in their assessments of themselves than they are of others. Even if that's not the norm, studies indicate that people who judge others without empathy are likely to do the same to themselves. So maybe we could all benefit from being kinder in this area.

We have to break free from self-consciousness and the spotlight effect to be comfortable and happy improvisers. Fortunately, there's a simple game, Kitty Wants a Corner, that addresses these phenomena, and it's my favorite to play at the start of a course or workshop. I learned it by a slightly different name in an improv course taught by Paul Sills, who was, among other noteworthy things, the original director of The Second City.

In Kitty Wants a Corner everyone in the group stands in a circle, save for one person who's in the middle. If you're in the circle, your goal is to trade places with others in the circle, which you do when you make eye contact with them. You want to trade places as many times as you can with as many other people as you can. If you're in the middle, your goal is to get out, stealing the spot of one of the others who is swapping places.

If you're in the middle, Kitty, chances are good that people will be hesitant to trade places if you stare at them forebodingly and cut off their angles of passage. Thus, Kitty creates a diversion by approaching people in the circle and saying, "Kitty wants a corner." The person approached responds with, "Go see my neighbor." There is no deep meaning (or any meaning at all, I suppose) here; it's just an interaction intended to make those behind Kitty's back feel safe enough to trade places and get the game going.

When Kitty nabs a spot, the person left without a spot becomes Kitty. You play until you don't feel like playing anymore. There is no score, no winners, no losers, no prizes. Sounds basic, huh? Yet there's so much more to this game than meets the eye.

Once, at the start of a new MBA term, I tried to get the class to play Kitty Wants a Corner, but we couldn't get the game started. No one moved. I was just walking around the circle, saying, "Kitty wants a corner" to people who might look at me but not at anyone else. Some of them looked at the ceiling, others at the floor.

So I stopped and said something like, "Well, I thought we might play a game and have a little fun, but if you insist on behaving like this is business school, then let's go that way instead. Let's do a case study of Kitty Wants a Corner, specifically a risk analysis." My intuition was that no one was playing because they felt the stakes were too high.

Our ensuing discussion might have been transcribed as follows.

> GREG: What's the worst that can happen in this game, barring severe injury or death, which have not occurred in the years I've been playing it, and I can therefore conclude are not likely?
> *Pause*
> STUDENT A: (*tentatively*): You get stuck in the middle.
> GREG: Of course, the construct of the game is to avoid or get out of the middle. If no one cares about that, then we don't have the tension required for the game. But aside from that construct, why is being in the middle bad?
> STUDENT B: It's embarrassing.
> GREG: Why?
> STUDENT C: Because you're the center of attention.
> STUDENT D: Because you're being judged.
> GREG: Okay, you might be in the center of the circle, but are you the center of attention? When you're on the perimeter, where is your focus?
> STUDENT E: On the people you're trying to trade with.
> GREG: That's certainly true for me. I have an awareness of Kitty, but that's not where most of my attention is. I'm thinking about *me* and what *I'm* trying to accomplish. *I* am the center of attention for me. As for the judgment, what are you thinking of Kitty? What a loser! How did that person even get into this school?
> *Scattered chuckles.*
> GREG: No, that's what you're thinking about yourself if you're Kitty.

After that we had a ripping good game of Kitty Wants a Corner with lots of risk-taking and laughter. No one was severely injured or killed.

So the good news, brothers and sisters, is that no one really gives a shit about you! Or perhaps a nicer way of saying that is no one notices all our little flaws and snafus as much as we do ourselves. We've got much more wiggle room than we realize.

If you're going to improvise well, onstage or off, you have to keep in mind that you're not the center of everyone else's world, and you've also got to be kind to yourself. There's enough stress and cruelty in the world without your adding more to it, directed at yourself or others.

Spotlight effect or no, just because people have self-interest doesn't mean that our loved ones don't love us or that no one notices us. I'm simply saying that we're all primarily concerned with ourselves and see the world from the perspective of "What does this have to do with me?" Considering that our audiences are, by default, self-interested, we have to work hard to get and keep their attention. Fortunately, we can do that better if we're not self-obsessed.

I'd like to conclude this section by mentioning three other things that may arise in Kitty Wants a Corner and that are good to keep in mind at the start of a workshop or course.

Control

Kitty sometimes tries to control the game by cutting off angles or jumping out of verbal exchanges with players to surprise other players. This behavior only makes the other players more hesitant to move. Kitty has to relax a little and trust that a spot will come open if Kitty gives it a chance. If you're Kitty and you try too hard, you're only prolonging your suffering.

This is the tip of the control iceberg we'll continue to discuss. Control is the enemy of successful improv. Control squelches spontaneity and only frustrates would-be controllers and controlees. Much better to learn to surf than to try to control the ocean.

Embarrassment

This game and much of what we do in improv has the potential to embarrass participants. Yes, there is potential for embarrassment about "losing" or "failing" in the game, but the activity itself might feel awkward for many.

For example, I was surprised to learn that some people are

embarrassed just saying the words, "Kitty wants a corner." After all, there's no real kitty present and no corner in a circle, and this all becomes odder if your first language isn't English. Just because I'm used to doing weird, potentially embarrassing things doesn't mean others are. My job is to be gentle and consider perspectives that might differ from mine.

Embarrassment is an emotional reaction, not an intellectual decision. Embarrassment is almost never extreme in class, and a little bit can be a good thing if it's part of raising one's threshold of embarrassment and immunity to it.

Know the Difference Between Fear and Danger

We often recoil emotionally from something that doesn't present an actual threat to us. It's okay to feel fear, but we have the gift of reason to free us from the cage in which fear can imprison us. Understanding the difference between fear and danger is the key to analyzing risk. The best question I know to ask yourself when you're afraid is, "What's the worst that can happen?" Identify that, and then decide if you can live with it.

As for improv, well, we're not cliff-diving here (unless it's part of a scene we're playing). Improv might make you fearful and uncomfortable, but it almost certainly won't kill you.

What's the best that can happen? That's up to you.

Exercises

Individual

1. Recall a time when you were embarrassed. Now try to imagine it from the perspective of someone else. Would it be memorable or significant to that person?
2. Recall another embarrassing situation (or even the same one). Now imagine it as a scene in a comedy played by your favorite comic actor.
3. Try to recall a situation that was embarrassing for someone else. How do you feel about it? Is it a big deal to you?
4. What is the difference between playing and competing? Do you spend time doing either or both? If so, how?

Group

1. **Kitty Wants a Corner**
   A. Group stands in a circle with one person in the middle.
   B. People in the circle trade places when they make eye contact. Their goal is to trade places as many times as they can throughout the game.
   C. Person in the middle is Kitty, whose goal is to find an open spot when other players are trading places.
   D. Kitty creates a diversion to make other players feel safer and more likely to trade places. The diversion is that Kitty approaches people in the circle and says, "Kitty wants a corner." The person spoken to responds with, "Go see my neighbor."
   E. Make sure the players understand how to play, and then play as long as you like. If the game is not going well, stop and see if you and the group can figure out why.

2. **Sevens** (distance learning)
   Kitty Wants a Corner isn't a possibility if you aren't in person. During the COVID pandemic, Sevens became my go-to starter for exploring the spotlight effect, risk, and other topics in this chapter. Sevens works well with distance-learning applications such as Zoom and Teams, and it's also an excellent game in person.
   A. Break your group into subsets of five to seven persons. Use breakout rooms if you're online. Explain the game before you open the rooms.
   B. One person will start by giving another person a category, starting with the word "seven." Examples: Seven brands of breakfast cereal, seven European capitals, seven things you like to do on a Saturday, seven American automobile manufacturers that went out of business before World War II, seven things you would never say to your mother-in-law.
   C. That second person will give examples that fit the category. With each answer, the group says aloud what number that was ("Froot Loops." "ONE!" "Corn flakes." "TWO!" and so on).
   D. When person two has reached seven, they give person

three a new category who then gives seven examples while the rest of the group counts.

   E. Repeat until everyone has given a category to someone else and given seven examples for someone else's category. I like to give everyone two turns at each task for more active experience.

   F. IMPORTANT! There are no wrong answers in this game. It's not a trivia contest; any answer is sufficient, and the goal is to say it quickly. The category is breakfast cereals, and someone says, "Talinn?" That counts! Can't think of an example? Make one up; that counts! Just say seven things, and say them fast.

   G. Demonstrating this game is helpful. Have a participant give you a category. If it's an easy one, deliberately make a mistake. Seven types of soft drink? Hupmobile! If anyone tries to correct you or call you out, remind them that any answer counts. By the way, even the seemingly easiest categories can be challenging. Everyone can quickly spit out three examples, but four through seven can be toughies, and that's the point.

   H. During the game you might need to remind players— repeatedly—that any answer counts and that speed is the goal. You also might need to remind players passing judgment on the answers that any answer is valid.

   I. Process the game when you're done playing. Ask the players about their experience. Ask them why it's challenging. If they report feeling judged or pressured, ask them if judgment and pressure seemed to be coming from others or themselves.

When you're giving seven examples in this game, you will feel self-conscious and likely struggle, even though any example suffices. Why? To my mind, it's generally due to perceived societal pressure to be correct, the ego demanding that you show how smart and clever you are, or both. Both will hamper your ability to improvise and must be addressed before you start improvising.

Sevens also does a good job of establishing an improv paradigm in which something is always better than nothing. Accuracy is important in the real world, but to improvise well we need to step away from that in order to develop some other muscles.

2

Your Check-In Time

"Until you make the unconscious conscious, it will direct your life and you will call it fate."—Carl Jung

Care.

That was what I came up with when someone once asked me to condense improv into a single word. There are many important components in improv, but care has to be the motivator behind all of them. You care about your fellow players, the audience, and yourself. You care about your characters, scenarios, technique, impulses, and ideas.

And how do you show you care? You pay attention. You listen. You're aware. You focus on what really matters instead of your self-centered neuroses, such as the spotlight effect, which we addressed in the previous chapter.

You listen to others so you can react to and build upon their ideas. You listen to yourself so you can respond with intellectual and emotional honesty to what's happening. Being aware is more important than being clever or funny. In other words, being present is more important than being wonderful. But the exciting possibility is that being present can lead to being wonderful.

Listening is hard though. We get distracted and have so many thoughts and feelings racing through our heads. Conversations turn into dueling monologues because we spend time formulating what we want to say instead of truly listening to others.

Moreover, in our society we tend to think of good communicators as people who are skilled at *giving* information. But if we look at communication as an *exchange* of information, then receiving must be as good as giving.

Being a good listener requires practice. For that reason almost all my class sessions, workshops, rehearsals, and pre-show warm-ups devote time to listening. From the outside this practice might look like casual conversation, but it's a deliberate ritual, Check-In.

I was first exposed to the Check-In ritual in the early '90s by educator/artist Sheila Kerrigan, the author of *The Performer's Guide to the Collaborative Process*. She explained to my company that, at the start of a meeting, everyone in the room takes turns introducing themselves and telling everyone else how they're doing. Participants should avoid saying "Fine" because it's a conditioned, nearly meaningless response. Instead, they should be encouraged to relate how they're really feeling at that moment and perhaps that day or week.

Maybe you've had a bad day, and something is weighing on your mind, like a conflict with a partner. Maybe your pet is sick or you're just inexplicably crabby. Maybe you're euphoric about something great that's just happened and finding it hard to focus. Maybe you're tired or jittery or sick or giddy or whatever. Improv requires being present in the moment, and you don't want your emotional baggage keeping you from it. How you feel will affect your work, but it doesn't have to control it.

The facilitator might solicit additional Check-In information as well. For example, at the start of a course, I ask students what they hope and expect to get out of it. By the way, I like to start sessions with an active game before settling down for Check-In. An activity raises energy and creates a playful atmosphere, whereas sitting is more likely to create stasis.

Shortly after my company learned about Check-In and began using it regularly, one of my brothers was getting married. He had a bachelor party in Baltimore two days before the wedding, and on the intervening day I needed to return to North Carolina for a performance. I made the trip on my motorcycle.

When I returned from the party for the show, I was none too fresh. In fact, I was exhausted. But I remember just saying to myself, "Okay, you're tired," and then setting it aside. I wound up having a great show, as did the company, and found an energy that was different from what I would normally have for a performance. Had I not taken the time to acknowledge my fatigue, I think I would have been disoriented by rather than comfortable with it.

Improv is all about going with what you have rather than wishing for what you don't, and that includes your states of mind, heart, and body.

Speaking of motorcycling, whenever I head out on the bike, I check in with my emotional state. Motorcycling is a potentially dangerous activity. If I can't set aside my emotions and ride in a disciplined, rational manner, then I'm making it more dangerous. Some unnoticed anger could make me impatient or provoke road rage. Being tired or spacy can make me less alert. Of course, you don't have to ride a motorcycle or even be going anywhere or doing particularly anything to make a practice of Check-In.

Check-In is part of learning to listen to yourself, being aware of your reaction to the world around and inside you. As much as you must pay attention to others in improv, you must pay attention to yourself. That initial response you have to a person, situation, or thing is the most honest and personal you can have. So notice it. You don't have to *act* on it, but pay attention to it. Your vast array of reactions is part of what makes you unique and inherently valuable.

As for listening to others, there's more to it than just being able to respond to what they say and do. Listening (or paying attention) is the first step in forming a connection with someone else. Once you start listening to someone, you start to know them. Once you start to know them it's hard not to feel a connection with—and even affection for—them. That doesn't mean you'll like everything about them or agree with them all the time. We all have our flaws and shortcomings, but these are also the things that make us who we are, lovable and sometimes not so lovable.

In addition to "How are you?" there are endless themes to explore in Check-In. Some themes are simple, such as a movie or song title. Some are silly, like a gross incompetence (my all-time favorite, "not being able to figure out how shoes go back into the box"). Some run deeper, like something that scares you or someone you admire. All are potentially profound and/or funny, and I think it's best not to have an expectation that they be anything at all. The more that important issues can arise organically rather than through forced facilitation, the better. Relating how you have difficulty fitting shoes into a shoebox can be just as meaningful as telling about a grandparent who sacrificed for their family. The sharer not only gets the opportunity but also has the responsibility to speak and be heard, and the group learns about and thus connects to its members.

If you're facilitating a Check-In, insist that there be only one person talking at a time and no interrupting. Everyone must pay attention, and that means no phones or other distractions. Check-In isn't about fixing anyone or their issues but rather simply listening. As your group members become more familiar with each other, you'll find they have empathetic responses to each other's Check-Ins. This helps develop group understanding, cohesiveness, and trust.

In my business school classes I've had students report time and time again that they've gotten to know fellow students better than in any other class. Part of that is due to the experiential nature of the work, and part of it is due to Check-In. I've had students say that they didn't know it was possible to connect with people outside of their families or social circles the way they do through Check-In.

One student wrote:

> Never in my life have I felt more comfortable around a group of strangers in such a short amount of time. If you told me in January that I would be crawling around on the floor greeting my classmates as a sloth or crying in front of everyone while I told them about my cousin who was killed by a distracted driver, I would have called you a liar... [M]y peers became a family. We became a unit that was not afraid of being ourselves because of how accepting each and every person was. This is special.... Our classroom was a safe spot for trying new things or getting in touch with your emotions.

Another added:

> One of the most important lessons the people in this class taught me is to be accepting of all different types of people and to not make snap judgments. We all do this, and I may be a pretty bad culprit. When I first joined the class, I immediately tried to figure out who was who, what their "thing" was, how everyone acted, etc. I didn't at first think I would get along with everyone. I actually decided that I wouldn't like certain people in the class. A lot of my quick assumptions and judgments came from a fear that other people were thinking the same thing about me; that they wouldn't like me or had already stereotyped me into the person they thought I was.... As I got to know everyone, I learned how talented and unique each person in the class was.... Also, the people who are the most different from you may end up teaching you the most.

Heartwarming though those testimonials are, there are more concrete reasons for having groups know each other. Research shows that when members of a team feel connected and like each other, the team is more efficient and productive.[3] A connected group should be able to reduce conflict and handle it better when it does arise, because there's greater shared understanding and disagreements are less likely to be personal.

Check-In might not initially feel like "work" or an efficient use of time. It also might seem too "touchy-feely," but that's actually its purpose, and I have no compunction about saying so and laughing about it. Transparency and a sense of humor are great assets in the classroom. I believe the process of getting to know and connect to others cannot be rushed and is ultimately very worthwhile. I've had eager and impatient people in various settings tell me that they eventually understood the purpose of Check-In even if at first it seemed a waste of time.

And I reiterate that Check-In is practice for paying attention, a manifestation of what I feel is the most important aspect of improv, caring. Listening is a key to getting outside of your head and getting into the moment and connection with others. You can't practice it too much.

That said, Check-in can last longer than you planned or expected. That can be okay because it could mean your group is bonding. But if you want a shorter Check-In, you can impose limitations to shorten the process. I try to make my limitations playful, like keeping the speaker to just three words or five seconds. You can still express a lot in a short time.

Check-In also serves as practice for extemporaneous speaking. Over the years I've often had students tell me that the more they checked in, the easier they found it and the less they found themselves planning exactly what to say. What's more, they said this increased comfort continued outside of class.

By the way, all those years ago Sheila Kerrigan also taught my company about Check-Out, in which you summarize your group's session. Check-Out helps the group identify, individually and collectively, what it learned and accomplished. It might involve every participant speaking, or it might pose a question like, "What are five useful things from today?"

On the final day of courses, I use Check-Out as Check-In and ask, "What's something you've gotten from this course?" This ritual is usually a profound, moving, educational, and gratifying experience. And crazy as it sounds, I hear students begin their Check-Out by saying, "Well, first I want to say that I love you guys."

Pay attention to yourself, and share it. Pay attention to others, and be sensitive to them. Care. Everything you do—in and out of improv—depends on it.

Exercises

Individual

1. **Check-In**
   A. What's on your mind right now? What are you feeling?
   B. The next time you're getting ready to do something challenging, take a moment to notice your thoughts and feelings. Think of it as cleaning out clutter from your head because you'll need the space for the challenge.
   C. As part of the previous step, notice if you're telling yourself stories about past or future performances. Are you psyching yourself out? Can you set aside past failures and anxiety about the future and focus on readiness and technique?

2. **Echo Listening**
   See the description for group Echo Listening below. This is essentially the same except that you are in the role of listener rather than speaker. You can practice aloud with a friend or family member if they're willing. You can also try the exercise in secret, echoing the speaker's words in your mind as they say them. Just be prepared to have it feel strange at first and also to have the speaker ask you what's up because you'll seem so attentive (or your lips are moving).

Group
(Both can be used in virtual environments as well as in person.)

1. **Check-In**
   A. Sit or stand in a circle or oval. Circles are good for engendering democratic environments. Where we sit or stand in a room and in relation to each other and the furniture says a lot about hierarchy and perceived power.
   B. Everyone gets a chance to speak and everyone has to speak, even if it's just a little. If you're leading the group, go first (at least the first time) to mitigate pressure. Proceed in order around the circle just so there's no confusion about who goes next. If you're online rather than in person, you can pass or "popcorn" to the next speaker by calling their name. You can even turn this

into a game of imaginary catch by checking in and then saying, "I'll pass a purple grape to So and So." Mime the toss and have the recipient mime the catch. When they've checked in, they can toss a red brick or a bowl of soup or whatever to the next person. You can also have people who haven't checked in yet raise their hands so that the speaker knows where to pass next.

C. You might mention that there is no need to entertain or say something "good."

D. Make sure there are no interruptions. If others want to comment, ask them to wait until the end of the individual check-in or the entire session.

E. The more you do this, the easier it gets. Some people might think it's corny at first, and they have good reason for thinking that. But stick with it, and make it a ritual. There's nothing corny about paying attention to yourself and others.

2. **Echo Listening**

A. Stand in front of your group, and tell them that you would like them to start saying the words you're saying, aloud, when you say "go." Say "go," and then you can say pretty much anything; perhaps tell the group about your morning or something that happened to you recently.

B. The group should be saying what you're saying at this point, and, if they're not, tell them they should be.

C. Once everyone is speaking along with you, throw in something unexpected, like announcing that you're a platypus, not only to keep the listeners on their toes but also to illustrate how we often make assumptions and finish others' sentences.

D. After 20–30 seconds, tell the group that they should now stop saying aloud the words you're saying and should instead just say them in their heads.

E. After another 20–30 seconds, tell the group that they can stop echoing all your words in their heads—if they can.

F. Ask the group how it went. You'll likely hear that the exercise was distracting or even disturbing. Some people might say they lost track of meaning. That's okay because this is merely a practice for refocusing your attention.

G. You'll want to stress that this is sort of an intervention activity and not the same as active listening. If one finds one's mind wandering in a discussion, one can employ this Echo Listening technique (the silent version!) to reconnect with the other participant(s) in the conversation. Once the connection is reestablished and your mind has stopped wandering, you can discontinue.

H. You'll notice when you're leading the exercise that the audience seemed extremely attentive, and you should tell them that, that you felt heard. Ironically, your audience might not have comprehended what you were saying even though they were paying attention. This is worth discussing.

I. Emphasize that, as with any new technique, this will feel awkward and distracting until you get used to it. Don't try it for the first time in a high-stakes situation but rather create opportunities for practice.

3

Rip to Connect

"We do not see things as they are, we see things as we are."—Anaïs Nin

Improv involves connecting with other people. This connection is the biggest difference between improv and mere ad-libbing, which is more of a solo act. If you want to improvise well, onstage or off, you need to pay attention and connect to other people, going beyond mere listening even to the extent of imagining yourself in others' places.

In improv onstage we have to see our partners as resources for what we're trying to achieve rather than as obstacles to it. If you pay attention to your partner(s) and they pay attention to you, you will discover something. If you support them and they support you, you can trust each other and find your way out of any jam or at least not have to endure it alone. We just have to avoid disconnecting and spinning around inside our heads with distressing thoughts about how this isn't working and never will and dammit why don't people *like* me more.

In decades of seeing and being in improv scenes that didn't work, I'd say that the unifying theme was lack of connection between the players. Instead of players working together as a team, you have separate entities working independently of and even in opposition to each other. Lack of connection kills improv. Yet I've seen and been in many scenes that were saved by connection. The content of the scene might have been a disaster, but somehow it worked because the players were in it together, playing and making the best of a bad situation.

The radical paradigm shift in improv is that it's all about your partner, not you.

The disconnect that happens in improv can happen in professional situations with similarly negative consequences. I've had it happen to me more than once. I can remember discussing a proposal with a potential client and having my mind wander off and start spending the money I hadn't yet earned. Then I found myself disconnected and unaware of what was going on. Fortunately, I reconnected and landed the gig, but it was a learning experience.

As a presenter and teacher, I've become distracted by self-evaluation or some other non-helpful thought and again had to escape my solipsism and reestablish a connection with others.

The improviser's faith is that no matter what happens in a situation, the solution is present if we can maintain awareness and remain open to it. Just as your partner is your best resource in a scene, so your client or colleague is your best resource in a professional situation. Pay attention to them, and the answer will reveal itself. Or it won't—but at least it won't be because you were trapped within your own thoughts and ego.

Rip Van Winkle, named for the eponymous Washington Irving short story, is an exercise that's very good for connecting people, especially nonperformers. I first saw this exercise demonstrated by Stevie Ray (the Minneapolis improviser, not the late Texas bluesman), although I don't know whether or not he invented it.

The premise is that you have a person, Rip, who has been asleep for 200 years (not just 20, as in the original story) and just awakened today. Rip's partner is going to explain something from our modern world in terms that Rip can understand. Let's use email or texting as an example.

I'm writing this in 2021, and 200 years ago there were not only no personal computers but also no typewriters (and thus typewriter keyboards), and electricity wasn't controlled in such a way as to power computers or other electronic devices. There were no telephones and therefore no telephone wires, to say nothing of wireless networks. Most of us are very familiar with computers, smart phones, and their accouterments, but imagine trying to explain them to someone who has no idea what they are. The same is true of so much other modern technology.

In this exercise you can't successfully describe email by saying, "Well, you turn on your PC or Mac, and once it's booted you click on the app with your mouse and then start typing what you want. You know, the words are on the screen, and you can edit before you send it. You might want to run spell check." To someone from 1821, those sentences would be gobbledygook. Hell, to someone from 1981 most of it would be.

Before you go into all the details of email, you might want to consider why you are using it at all. I remember the first time I heard about email and thinking it sounded futuristic. I recall being unsure of how your email address worked and how messages even found you. Cool though it seemed, I wasn't convinced of its value to me. Then I realized I could communicate with someone far away instantly and without having to use paper, ink, or stamps. I could even edit my message or correct errors without having to retype the whole thing.

In other words, once I saw the benefit of this new technology, I was eager to use it even though I didn't—and don't—understand precisely how it works or many of its features. I value so many things without having complete understanding of them. I couldn't build or even repair a microwave oven, but I sure like being able to heat up a cup of coffee in one.

In this exercise, most participants in the role of explainer begin by focusing on the features, the hows, to Rip rather than the benefits, the whys. There is so much technological progress to explain that the explainers often make things more confusing than clearer.

So you have someone describe email by saying something like, "There's a magical box that's powered by lightning. You push these buttons [a term that would only apply to clothing 200 years ago] and letters appear on a screen, and then they're sent to someone invisibly by miniature horses." While this might be a fine opium-induced vision (something that did exist in 1821), it's not a very clear explanation of how email works or why someone might want to use it.

Seeing as we've examined our self-interested nature in a previous chapter, let's look at benefits as a way of tapping into someone else's self-interest. What does all this mean and what can it do for *them*? Once they've seen that, they might not care about the features, and, if they do, their attention and understanding will be higher because their self-interest is engaged. That said, be aware that what is a benefit to you might not be to someone else.

Some of you readers will quickly see, just as many of the students have, how this approach applies to sales. "Sales" is almost a dirty word because some salespeople employ manipulation and trickery.

But if salespeople took the approach of an educator sharing potential benefits, that might well lead to more—and better—sales. If your client is satisfied and has no buyer's remorse, that can lead to repeat business as well as referrals. This is a happier and more sustainable approach than the zero-sum, rip-off-and-run school of sales.

Whatever the situation might be, put yourself in the position of your counterpart or audience. Think of how what you're saying might seem to them instead of how it already seems to you. This focus will help your audience understand you on an intellectual level.

Putting yourself in others' shoes (metaphorically at least) is also known as empathy. You imagine what it'd be like to be someone else, show you care, and treat them as you would wish to be treated. People talk about empathy as this new thing in the professional world, but when has it not been a good idea to care about your clients and colleagues and to demonstrate that concern? Empathy fosters understanding on emotional levels and complements intellectual understanding.

Another benefit of focusing on others is that it takes pressure off you. You don't have to solve problems and innovate in an egoistic vacuum. Instead, you have a partner or partners, and the unexpected alchemy between and among you can take you where you couldn't have gone by yourself. You're not solely responsible for the process! This is as true for when you're making up scenes as when you're actually living them.

Incidentally, if you're practicing or experimenting with applied improv, you're already essentially playing Rip Van Winkle. You can drop catchy improv terms like "yes and" all day long, but those are just features unless you can translate them into beneficial offstage techniques. Invite your audience to ask questions if they don't understand you; it's much more important that they comprehend your message than that you present it seamlessly.

"[T]he creative life is the greatest life," writes Jon Snyder, Chair of Film & Music Industry Studies in New Orleans. "It is full of rewards, but it is also full of suffering. I understand that. But by dedicating yourself to these kinds of values, the payoff down the road, for the individual and the whole culture, is tremendous. The old model of working independently and in isolation is dead. The future is about connection."[4]

Get out of your head and get into someone else's. You might enjoy the change of scenery.

Exercises

Individual

1. Remember a time when you felt overwhelmed by something you didn't understand. Maybe it was algebra or a smart phone. How did not understanding make you feel? Did you understand the benefits of this new thing?
2. Think of some modern technology. Setting aside how it works, make a list of all the ways it can help you. Try this with a few products and/or services.
3. Again, disregarding feasibility, think of a need or desire you have and an invention that could fill it.
4. Think about a disagreement you've had. What did you want out of the situation? What did the other person want? Did the disagreement focus on those issues, or did it turn into an interpersonal conflagration?
5. Think about a time when you just weren't paying close enough attention to someone to understand what that person wanted or needed. Or maybe your needs or desires weren't understood. How might you communicate differently now?

Group

Rip Van Winkle

A. Divide your group into twos, and have each pair split into Rip and Friend. If you have an uneven number, have a threesome start with two Friends and one Rip. Mention that you will play the game twice so that everyone will play both roles. Rip has just awakened after a 200-year nap.
B. Explain that the Friends will explain something from our modern world in terms that the Rips can understand. Give examples of current things and terminology that didn't exist 200 years ago. Rip should assume good intent on the part of Friend, but if Rip doesn't understand what Friend is saying, Rip should ask questions. Finally, give the group something to explain, like email, a microwave oven, or an airplane.
C. Set aside three minutes for Friend's first explanation to Rip. Afterward ask some of the Rips to tell the rest

of the group what the modern thing is, based on the explanation they just received.

D. You will probably hear a lot of features but few benefits. There might be some laughter, and some of the Friends might wind up wearing sheepish grins. Ask the Rips how many of them want this new technology, and then ask them why or why not.

E. Discuss the difference between features and benefits. Are there secondary or even tertiary benefits to the new technology? For example, email and texting are instant, but they can also file your correspondence without taking up literal space. You can send the same letter to many people. You can attach files. The list can become quite long.

F. Are the benefits relevant to Rip? For example, one couldn't assume in 1821 that everyone was literate. Maybe Rip lives mere minutes away from everyone Rip knows.

G. If anyone complains that three minutes was too short for an adequate explanation, suggest that tapping into someone's self-interest needs to happen early in a discussion.

H. Discuss the experience of the exercise. What was challenging? What was rewarding? How could it go better?

I. Have the participants switch roles and repeat the exercise with the Friends explaining a different modern thing. Instruct the new Friends to try to apply what they learned as Rip to their new role as Friend. Instruct them to focus on Rip and Rip's needs as well as on benefits rather than features.

J. Stop the explanations after three minutes, and again ask the Rips to tell us what the modern thing is based on the explanation they just heard. See how many Rips are interested in this new thing. Was the second explanation process different from the first? If so, how?

K. Finish processing the exercise by exploring real-world takeaways. Your players should be able to identify some, but, if not, try suggesting sales pitches, job interviews, and conflict resolution for starters.

4

Laying the Groundwork

Finding Your FIZ

"There are enough closed doors and glass ceilings in the world. My comfort zone shouldn't be one of them."
—Joya Goffney

Unless you're looking to become an onstage performer, one of your main reasons for studying improv is probably to expand your comfort zone. Good for you! Just keep in mind that you're the only person who can do this work for you. Someone else might be able to help or to create the circumstances in which it happens, but you'll have to do the heavy lifting.

The only way I know to expand your comfort zone is to get out of it. You have to court what you want to avoid, making yourself feel uncomfortable or maybe even like a complete fool. It's akin to how athletes work themselves to exhaustion and weakness in order to build stamina and strength.

By venturing outside of your comfort zone, you're likely to encounter feelings of confusion, incompetence, embarrassment, and shame, among other things. And yet you'll find that none of these emotions is immediately fatal or even very harmful—although the deleterious, long-term effects of emotional stress have been well documented by science.

Improv activities can cause anxiety. You might be doing something as simple as improvising an abstract gesture, and yet you experience an elevated pulse rate, sweating, and shortness of breath. With repetition, however, these responses diminish. You become desensitized and can improve your ability to handle embarrassment and stress.

At the end of courses, I like to reprise an exercise or two from the beginning so that students realize just how far they've come. Through repeated forays outside their comfort zones, students claim new territory that was once the realm of discomfort and is now a bigger comfort zone. Students have to take the first step though, as well as the steps that follow. No one can teach them that experience; they must live it for themselves.

My Kenan-Flagler MBA students came up with a term for the border between the areas of comfort and discomfort, action and stasis. They called it "the Fuck-It Zone" (or FIZ if you prefer a more polite and effervescent acronym).

You know how you've straddled the fence between doing something daunting and not doing it? Maybe you were trying to figure out how to ask out that special someone or working up the courage to jump off the high board at the swimming pool. Well, you probably reached the point where you tired of your indecision, said "fuck it," and just did it. You committed to a course of action instead of staying put or reversing.

That's a beautiful and exciting thing because you're opening yourself to growth and new horizons. The FIZ is the gateway to infinity, the limitlessness of yes. By contrast, your comfort zone is limited. Its border seems to offer safety from the unknown and the frightening, which is how opportunity and adventure appear from behind that line. That border not only keeps things out, but it also keeps you inside.

In my classes I often have students give spontaneous speeches with the goal of conveying an emotional message. If speakers are only hinting at the emotions, I'll push them out of their comfort zones by having them exaggerate or emote. Sometimes students object, saying, "That's just not me." I see their point, but that's not *the* point.

I want these reticent and tentative people to burst through the FIZ and out of their comfort zones. I want them to risk appearing foolishly enthusiastic about seemingly inconsequential things like cookies or shoes so that they can bring that same fervor to truly important things like justice, love, and their dreams. I want them to go "too far" and be surprised by the positive and enthusiastic reactions they invariably receive. Heartily expressing your emotions not only helps your audience to understand your message but also to share your passion.

What seems like outlandish exaggeration to the speaker from their interior perspective usually seems just right and *real* to the audience from its exterior perspective. And because speakers *can* go over the top, they don't necessarily need to do so because they somehow convey that potential, texture, and depth. I don't know why this is, but I've seen it often enough in speakers, actors, and singers.

After leaping through the FIZ and surviving it, the next step is practicing. With repetition, what once seemed outrageously risky and scary becomes a matter of course. Part of that is familiarity, and part of it is increasing expertise. You learn and improve with practice.

You'll still make mistakes, but, because your comfort zone is bigger, the mistakes won't get to you like they once did. Your comfort zone might become so big that others might never even be aware or care that you're making mistakes. (This is not an argument for being unprepared, incompetent, indifferent, and dishonest but rather one for letting confidence and comfort enhance your honest hard work.) You might even realize how a lack of commitment to a course of action, doing something halfway, can cause failure.

Accepting and getting past mistakes is crucial in improv and probably everywhere. It seems to me that people are most likely to fail when they're worrying primarily about not failing rather than about succeeding. That's what sportscasters mean when they say a team or player is "playing not to lose" rather than "playing to win."

I prefer "playing to play." Most of my classes begin with a silly game. Sometimes there are potentially deep takeaways from the game, but often my goal is simply for us to loosen up and have fun. There are no prizes or awards at stake. Yet most students, at least early in a course, are focused on winning the game rather than merely playing and having a good time.

Hey, I like to win too. Victory can be very gratifying. But it seems we adults lose the ability we had as children to *play* and wind up knowing only how to *compete*. Process-oriented playing changes into result-oriented competing. Fun can become pressure as players become contestants. Don't mess up; you might lose!

Our society inculcates us with the need to compete and to win. This isn't all bad, but at its extreme it engenders a desperate aversion to losing. Life, however, isn't a competition, and mistakes aren't defeat. Fear of losing can cause stagnation because we become unwilling to risk making mistakes and stick to the known. "Better a known devil than an unknown angel" is a Nigerian proverb that describes the outlook many of us have.

To my mind, stagnation and stasis are worse than defeat. If you're not making mistakes, you're not trying hard enough (a saying that has been attributed to numerous individuals, including Evan Davis and Vince Lombardi). If you want to improve as a tennis player, you have to play with people who are better at it than you are, which is just another way of saying you have to lose to improve. This principle applies to much more than just tennis.

Regardless, if you want to get better at something, you have to do it a lot. In doing it a lot you must do it wrong and learn from your mistakes. That we learn from our mistakes more than we do from our successes is a timeworn truism. Everyone's got a good war story about learning how to do something, whether it's parallel parking, public speaking, or dating. Chances are we learned from those mistakes and didn't repeat them. If we hadn't made the mistakes, we wouldn't have learned so well.

Beyond that, however, is the possibility of the sublime or transcendent mistake. History is littered with examples of artists and inventors finding themselves in a place better than the one where they'd planned to go. Good improvisers know this and welcome the "divine error," a mistake that is not a mistake but is rather something unplanned and unexpected that takes them far beyond what they had intended. Just because you didn't mean to do it, doesn't mean it's wrong!

Improv demands that you go beyond the known—beyond security and the ego—in order to excel. You have to do it *well* and not just *right*. So, when I'm teaching and directing, I encourage players to abandon what they know, their bag of tricks, and explore the unknown. The process is often disorienting and might feel wrong for the player, but results can be stunning.

Now I'm not suggesting that you deliberately try to be wrong but rather that the true measure of a person isn't whether or not they make mistakes but how they handle them.

Feeling at ease being and sharing yourself, mistakes and all, is the comfort zone to seek. If your comfort zone is less than that, it's not as safe as you think, and it's limiting you.

Exercises

Individual

1. Identify three risks you took that turned out well.
2. Identify three risks you took that didn't turn out well. How bad was the damage? What did you learn?
3. Identify three mistakes you made or misfortunes you experienced that wound up benefiting you.
4. Next time you're in the shower or car or somewhere somewhat private, sing a favorite song just like the singer would in concert. We all know you're not that singer, but just let it rip and focus on the feelings, not the notes.
5. Think of a time when you really wanted to express an emotion to someone. Say it aloud to yourself in a private place. If it's possible and seems right, say it to that person.
6. Imagine you had as much money as you wanted; what's something you'd do? Now imagine you were indestructible; what's something you'd do?

Group

1. **Samurai** (can be played in person or virtually)
    A. The group stands in a circle. (With distance-learning apps, just make sure everyone has their camera and microphone turned on and their screen set to gallery view.)
    B. The leader holds both hands above their head and then rapidly moves them toward someone, as if swinging a sword straight toward them, while making a loud and hearty samurai shout. (On screen, the leader calls the name of the person before making the gesture and shout.)
    C. The recipient "catches" the gesture, bringing their hands above their head and responding with a shout.
    D. The recipient's immediate neighbors slash at the recipient's waist with their imaginary swords while making a samurai shout. This causes the recipient to repeat the leader's movement and sound in step one. (Neighbors aren't involved in the remote-learning version. Instead, the recipient simply calls out

someone else's name and sends them the gesture and shout.)

E. Repeat until you feel like stopping. If the players show a lack of enthusiasm, try to encourage them, perhaps by telling them that they're simply not going to get cast in the Kurosawa film about samurais unless they give more energy.

F. The more energy you put into the game, the better you feel and the more the energy spreads among the players. It's super simple and super silly, but it also touches on super-deep principles. There's really nothing to Samurai except the commitment and energy the group brings to it.

2. **Questions**. The questions for individuals above can certainly be used for group discussion.

5

Getting FIZical

"There is more wisdom in your body than in your deepest philosophy."—Friedrich Nietzsche

My approach to improv is physical. Improv onstage is inherently corporeal in that we have a presence in the space, both literally in the theater as well as in the setting of the scene. Much of what we convey as players is physical. The players and audience alike get a sense of who the characters are by the way they move and sound. (Yes, I count sound as physicality.)

Good improvisers are physically expressive. They communicate so much without having to speak. Presence and movement are essential to good scenes. Without those two elements, you tend to have static "talking head" scenes. Those often devolve into mere clever contests, which are usually terrible because most of us aren't that clever. We remember the funny things Oscar Wilde said, even though he died in 1900, because his wit was rare.

Earlier I stated that most failed improv scenes are due to lack of connection among the players. Second place on my reasons-for-failure list is lack of physicality. Therefore, when I'm directing and coaching improv, I often encourage players to find a signature gesture or voice for their characters or to find some object in the space with which to interact. At the very least it makes the characters and scene more dynamic and interesting.

There's potentially much more to being physically engaged. Director/teacher Mick Napier once suggested to me that we remember our worst improv scenes because we're trapped in our analytical mind, which is good at remembering but bad at improv, and forget our best scenes because we're in our creative mind, which is good at improv but bad at remembering. He felt physicality was the key to unlocking the creative mind, and he's not alone in that belief.[5]

For the reasons above, I feel that everyday improvisers off the stage need to be physically aware and engaged. Doing so makes you a better presenter and communicator. It can also open you up to greater creativity. Walking meetings and other physically active work practices are not only growing in popularity but also gaining scientific credence.[6]

For most adults, physical activity means working out, competitive sports, or yoga, to name a few things. Those are all great—I regularly engage in them myself—but they can also be pretty serious and strenuous. I mean we call it "working out," not "playing out," right?

Focusing on theatrical physicality can also be daunting and awkward. Most of us don't have a lot of practice with this kind of work, and it can have us racing past self-awareness, a constructive thing, to self-consciousness, a destructive thing. Fortunately, that discomfort can be eased with improv's playful approach.

So many improv activities are physical and yet essentially child's play. We can engage and explore our bodies in ways that are light-hearted and even goofy. Most improv games aren't serious in and of themselves, and that's one reason why they can be used to address serious issues.

The introduction to physicality I generally use is the children's game Red Light, Green Light. It's played throughout the world, and I know because, over the years, my international students have told me its name in their home countries. In Mexico it's "One-Two-Three *Pumpkin!*" In Israel it's "One-Two-Three *Salt-Fish!*"

No matter what you call it, the game is pretty simple. Everyone in the group lines up against a wall or some other boundary. One person, "It," stands opposite the group, perhaps 20–30 feet (seven to ten meters) away. The goal for the people in the line is to reach and tag It without having It see them move. If It sees someone move, It sends that person back to the start to try again.

Fortunately, there's more to Red Light, Green Light than just that, which would make for a very long and slow game. To give the people in the line a fighting chance, It turns its back to them and says, "Green light," giving the other players the opportunity to advance toward It. At random intervals, It says, "Red light," and quickly turns back toward the other players. The players at this point try to freeze, and It tries to catch them moving. When someone reaches and tags

It, they become It and the group plays again. You play until you decide you've had enough but at least long enough to see that the players are getting better at freezing and unfreezing.

When I introduce this game, I point out that it's about action, not intention. Whether or not a player *intends* to move is irrelevant; it's the movement itself that counts. If you're moving and I'm It, I'll send you back.

"Even blinking your eyes?"

"Even blinking your eyes."

"Even chewing gum?"

"Even chewing gum."

And despite that thorough introduction, I still get a look of utter disbelief the first time I send someone back for blinking their eyes or chewing gum or twitching their fingers. "Whaaaaaat?!" Their reactions make me feel how basketball and soccer referees must feel after calling a foul.

When we're done playing, I ask the players why we're playing this game in business school or in a professional or executive workshop. To break the ice? Sure. To have fun? Yeah. To experiment with risk? Why not. To spur hatred for the instructor and anyone else who winds up being It? Maybe not so much but whatever.

My main reason for playing the game is for us to get familiar with what we're doing physically. I want everyone to be aware and in control of their bodies. You have to do that to win at Red Light, Green Light. And you have to do that if you're going to be a winning presenter or actor. Awareness and control are the prerequisites to being deliberate, dynamic, and authoritative. This is where "executive presence" starts.

Our next physical activity contains solo improvisation and an element of performance. Up to this point in the course everyone has done activities more or less simultaneously. This is a good way to build confidence. In addition, experiencing the unknown—to say nothing of the weird—anonymously goes a long way to making it less traumatic.

Let's face it though; the thrill and appeal of (or aversion to) improv is largely based on isolation and pressure, being put on the spot. What are these people onstage going to do with no plan? Maybe you're one of those people!

For all of improv's popularity, there are still a lot of people who haven't seen it or who have and don't really understand what's going on. They'll confuse stand-up or something they've seen on TV or in films with improv. Those things might be wonderful, but they're generally not only scripted but also pretty well refined by the time they reach an audience. Moreover, they've probably been written, produced, and performed by experienced people. That's why it's so important to give improv students a chance to do actual improvising early in their education. The experience can be exhilarating, and it can also be uncomfortable and difficult.

The exercise I call Gesture Circle goes by many names and is one of the most common improv activities. It's one of the first I ever experienced. It's also one of the first I use in classes and workshops because it's simple yet endlessly challenging and even entertaining. If you bring it back at the end of a course, it dramatically illustrates how far individuals and the group have come since the course began.

As with most improv exercises, Gesture Circle begins with the group standing in a circle. (Work with a group in improv long enough and they'll just automatically assemble in a standing circle when the leader says, "Let's get started"; it's a natural phenomenon.) The leader does an abstract, meaningless gesture to the next person in the circle. That person mirrors the movement back once the leader has finished and then turns to the next person and does a new abstract gesture, which is mirrored by that person, and so on. You'll want to go around the circle at least twice and maybe a few times.

My introduction for this exercise goes something like this: "Now we're going to get a chance to *improvise*. Seeing as this is an improv class and not a choreography class, *what* you do isn't nearly as important as *how* you do it."

I explain the mechanics of the activity as well as the term "abstract, meaningless gesture." In this activity, the participants shouldn't know what they're doing until they do it. A familiar movement automatically removes the possibility of discovery. Therefore, I suggest to my students that they avoid dance steps and miming everyday or athletic activities.

"Feel welcome to plan your movement," I'll continue. "Your mind's going to want to do that anyway, so let it. But when it gets to be your turn, do something other than what you've planned."

No matter how much I emphasize that last point, some players will still play it safe and do what they planned. Or they'll want to be funny and do a funny movement they've seen someone else do. Or they'll want to outdo their partner and do something really difficult, like a stunt or feat of strength.

All that's okay because the exercise is about learning, not mastery. I remind myself that the participants are only doing these things because the exercise is kind of scary, and they want to excel. I remind the players that the goal is to improvise and that they don't have to do it well; it's enough just to do it. What they come up with might not feel great, but coming up with anything at all is a triumph.

One last thing I mention is that the players don't have to worry about blanking and having no idea of what to do. That might well happen, especially for the most courageous players, but if they can be aware, then they'll always have something. They're supposed to initiate the next movement and they're stuck? They just need to notice their position and move something. This is building directly off the skills participants have developed in Red Light, Green Light.

Once the exercise is underway almost any group is having fun and laughing, giddy even. I'm often amazed by how enthusiastically players receive the game, but then I've been playing it for decades, and some of the bloom is off the rose. For most of the players though, this will be their first time playing Gesture Circle. Encourage them if they need it. Gently guide them back to the game if they're straying into something different.

I process the activity after we've gone around once if the group seems to be very uncomfortable or struggling, or twice if it seems to be going well. How is it going for them? Are they satisfied with what they're doing? What's challenging? Are there movements that they really liked or that the group responded strongly to? Why? I listen.

One thing I'm likely to hear is that it was hard for the participants not to plan. I remind them that it's okay to plan, just not to *do* what they planned. I congratulate them. They're improvising!

If there were gestures that elicited strong reactions (usually laughter), I'll ask people why. William Wordsworth wrote, "We murder to dissect," and usually dissecting why something is funny thoroughly kills the comedy. However, the important point here is that it's almost always *how* a gesture is performed rather than *what* it is that causes the big response. The most successful movements aren't subtle spoofs of Martha Graham or gestures that mock the economic principles of Milton Friedman; no, they're just gonzo, filled with gusto. A baby or maybe even an animal would get the humor.

Strong reactions indicate a cathartic release, and that's worth mentioning. We not only want to see each other do well, but we also crave the connection and, well, *joy* that ensues when someone really goes for it. "Catharsis" is a grand word with Greek roots. That seems appropriate seeing as how the ancient Greeks were masters of eliciting catharsis in their theater, both comedy and tragedy. The opposite of catharsis is an uncomfortable suppression and stifling, a feeling no one wants.

After the processing pause, I like to reverse the direction in which the movement travels and add sound—non-lingual, naturally, because we don't want our players to know what they're doing—to the movements.

Just before our final trip around the circle, I make sure everyone knows they have one last chance to really go for it in this game. I like to joke—only it's not really a joke—that if they're tentative and give only 35 percent that it will haunt them, and they'll spend hours and days wondering why their commitment was so paltry and thinking of better efforts they could have made. Conversely, if the players go all out, they'll simply feel good about the exercise and themselves rather than ruminating about both. I tell them, "You can strut out the door saying, 'Hey, I did some weird shit!'" This exhortation seems to work pretty well.

In the final go-round, compliment those who are going for it or who are showing improvement. If a player makes an unenthusiastic gesture, I often say, "Wonderful! Now do it again, but double the energy." If the player still struggles, I'll invite the whole group to do the gesture with the player. I want that player to feel supported, and I want that player—all the players—to succeed.

I'll often end class or go into a break after that last iteration of Gesture Circle with no more processing. We've already processed the exercise in the middle of it, and now we can stop at a high point and give participants a chance to reflect privately on their experiences.

One of the major improv concepts that this exercise introduces and illustrates is that success in improv is usually the result of going all out with whatever idea it is that you have rather than having a great idea. Leap before you look. Keep your foot off the brake, and gas it instead. Enter the FIZ.

Players are empowered and emboldened when they do those things. The message is, "You can do it." And nothing shows you can do it like doing it. Players also connect with each other in this exercise because they're not only playing together but also sharing each other's vulnerabilities and successes. Enthusiasm is contagious. So is being tentative.

Exercises

Individual

I just don't know how you can do these exercises in a solitaire version. It seems impossible to sublimate it into an everyday social interaction because it requires that you're put on the spot, both yourself and at least one other person. But it's not like you have to find a pro to play with. You can play with just about anyone who's willing, including and perhaps especially little children.

Group

1. **Red Light, Green Light** (Alas, I do not know how to play this game in a virtual environment.)
    A. Everyone in the group lines up against a wall or some other boundary.
    B. One person, "It," stands opposite the group, 20–30 feet (seven to ten meters) away.
    C. The people in the line try to reach and tag It without having It see them move. If It sees someone move, It sends that person back to the start to try again.
    D. To give the people in the line a fighting chance, It turns its back to them and says, "Green light," giving the other players the opportunity to advance toward It.
    E. At random intervals, It says, "Red light," before turning back toward the other players. The players try to freeze, and It tries to catch them moving. You might need to remind It—numerous times—that they need to say "Red light" *before*, not while, they turn around.
    F. When someone reaches and tags It, they become It, and the group plays again.
    G. Process the game. While I feel physicality is the main takeaway from the game, there will likely be other observations worth discussing.
2. **Gesture Circle**
    A. Group stands in a circle. (For distance learning, I like

to establish the order in which the participants go by making a list of their first names and posting it in chat. Make sure each player knows whom they're following and who's following them.)

B. Leader does an abstract movement (not mime, common dance move, or sign language) which leader's neighbor mirrors after leader has finished.

C. Neighbor does new abstract for next person in circle and so on. Each player mirrors and then creates a gesture.

D. Repeat as desired or necessary. Leader should look to encourage players and remind them not to do the movements they're planning but rather to improvise in the moment as that is the goal of the exercise.

E. Discuss. As always, the more the group can lead the discussion, the better (i.e., it's better to listen than to lecture, although the latter is most useful if no one's talking).

F. Restart exercise in opposite direction, and add sound to the gestures.

G. Repeat as desired or necessary. Leader should look to coach players toward greater commitment and energy.

3. **Flow Circle**
   This exercise is very similar to Gesture Circle except that the follower doesn't mirror the leader's movement but rather starts in the position where the leader stops and then makes a new movement to a new frozen position that is taken up by the next follower.

4. **Bring It Back**
   Gesture Circle and Flow Circle make for great warm-up exercises. They are also excellent to reprise at the end of a course, especially if you haven't played them since early in the course. No matter how you use them, having the players observe if or how the activity has changed for the individuals or the group can be very enlightening.

6

Focusing on Process

"Too much concern about how well one is doing a task sometimes disrupts performance by loading short-term memory with pointless anxious thoughts."
—Daniel Kahneman

Most of us want to do well at the things we attempt. We want to do them correctly. All our lives we're taught and encouraged to meet expectations and excel, whether it's getting good grades at school, winning at games, doing the right dance steps, or selling ideas and products at work. In improv, we probably want to get laughs. It's only natural that most of us are tempted to skip from the means to the ends, to be concerned more with the destination than the journey. The destination, however, is only the final part of the journey and not separate from it.

In improv the destination is *determined* by the journey because it's an exploration rather than a planned expedition. Indeed, you might go so far as to say that improv is the art of process because the performers travel the entire creative path, from ideation to execution, right in front of the audience.

In scripted theater the audience sees the end result but doesn't see the writing of the play and its evolution through the rehearsal process. The performers aren't creating the story as they go but are instead following a script. They can definitely make mistakes, such as saying the wrong lines or doing the wrong blocking. This isn't a criticism of scripted theater (of which I've done plenty as a professional and amateur), merely a comparison.

In improv, you can't really say or do *wrong* things the way you can in scripted theater because the scene you're doing doesn't exist yet; there is no external standard. You can use poor improv

46

technique, and part of that is thinking that your scene is supposed to go a certain way. You have to be open to discovery fueled by interactions with your fellow players.

Mary Pinard, a poet who has worked with business students at Babson College, talks about getting her students to "trust the form." She suggests that rather than worrying about where a poem will go and how it will end, you should work within the confines of your poetic form (sonnet, free verse, haiku, etc.), and the poem and its resolution will take care of themselves. This is also what prose writers mean when they talk about letting a story "write itself." The key here is that you have to write—engage in the process—in order for that to happen.

Likewise, when I assign term papers, I tell students to avoid *recounting* what they think they learned. Instead, I encourage them to relate their experience of the course and surprise both of us by *discovering* what they learned. This is focusing on process.

An old improv exercise I use regularly illustrates the danger of overlooking process and focusing solely on result. In this activity a small group of players secretly chooses three foods. Then, with the stated goal "Eat the imaginary foods," the players mime consuming them for the audience. After about 90 seconds, I ask the viewers to guess what the performers ate.

After all these years I find the exercise kind of boring to watch unless the players are really engaged and taking risks. You see, once the players realize that others are guessing what foods they're pretending to eat, they'll leapfrog the stated goal—to eat the imaginary food—and try to make the spectators correctly guess what the foods are. They pander to the audience and the exercise becomes a broad pantomime. Often I'll see players looking awkwardly at the audience, desperately needing its approval and understanding. No one wants to watch a needy performer.

However, we do want to watch self-possessed people deeply involved in what they're doing rather than trying to manipulate an audience and force an outcome. For example, Patrick, an MBA student of mine, once devoured an imaginary mango with such abandon that he made a virtual mess on his face, his hands, and the classroom floor. He was focused not on us but on what he was doing, and yet we *felt* what he was eating and didn't need to guess. We really didn't care what he was eating anyway because we were fascinated by him, what he was doing, and especially how he was doing it. We were engaged because he was engaged.

Incidentally, I'm not suggesting that we should be oblivious of our audiences. We should be sensitive and responsive but not slavishly beholden to them.

When we concentrate solely on outcome rather than process, we open ourselves up to the paralyzing trap of self-evaluation during performance, which is harmful, wasteful, and inaccurate. There's no way we can know whether or not we've achieved our desired result while we're in the middle of a scene, show, game, job interview, or sales pitch. We need all our energy and concentration to perform our task. Self-evaluation robs us of that energy and can dishearten us if we've decided we're failing. Legion are the stories of folks thinking they stank only to find they were succeeding—and vice versa.

When we're navigating an ambiguous situation—improvising—by definition we don't know where or how it's going to wind up. But if you concentrate on what you're doing now, the answers tend to reveal themselves when they become relevant and you need them. In improv we trust that we'll know what to do when we need to know it and not a moment beforehand. It's scary, but it's necessary and it works.

If focusing on process sounds like being present and in the here and now, it should. In many ways they're the same thing. Most of us are pretty familiar with the idea of being present. It's a concept that has gotten a lot of attention in recent decades even though it's one that goes back millennia, in Buddhism for example.

And speaking of Buddhism, there's a sutra that focuses on the "second arrow." The idea here is that there's the first arrow, which sucks because it's an arrow and it can hurt or kill you. The second arrow is the worry you have about the possibility of the first arrow, your subjective anxiety and suffering over the threat of an objective event. The second arrow is the "thousand deaths" we might suffer before our one actual death.

Once, in a bicycle race, I saw a hill ahead. *I'm going to suffer on that hill, and I might get dropped by the pack*, I thought. Then the concept of the second arrow occurred to me, and I figured I might as well suffer when I'm actually on the hill rather than beforehand when the going's still good. It turned out the hill looked a lot steeper from a distance than it really was, so I didn't get dropped or even suffer much. That came later.

Do you dread presentations? Interviews? Improv scenes? You might be experiencing the second arrow, and your energy could be better applied to preparation and focusing on process. Yes, that requires mental and emotional discipline, but it could result in increased effectiveness and decreased misery.

I have a suspicion that most people think "being present" is kind of boring. I mean, you have to be all quiet and mindful to be present, right? Well, that's only partially true. You might have heard of "peak" experiences, which psychologist Mihály Csíkszentmihályi refers to as "flow."[7] The experience might be something in nature, dancing at a party, live performance, or something extreme like rock climbing or skydiving. Whatever it is, you're so consumed by whatever you're doing that you're simply not thinking about anything else. It's like you're on vacation from yourself or at least that part of yourself that's always trying to be somewhere other than where you are.

Well, sure, if you're plummeting earthward, it's pretty easy to be in the moment. But what about those things that aren't quite so stimulating, like your everyday life or conversations? Elsewhere in this book, I talk about how good improvisers always have *something*, even if there doesn't seem to be anything, to go on. They're aware and they dig into what's happening around them. What is my partner doing? How am I moving or standing? What is my character feeling or thinking? And so it is offstage; you can always dig a little deeper and refocus on what's happening right now, which is also known as reality. Your thoughts about what isn't happening aren't reality.

I love peak experiences and try to have them as often as I can. I've found that I dissolve into the moment more than I used to. Perhaps that's practice, or maybe it's just maturation. Maybe it's both. I like objectively intense things like riding a motorcycle on twisty mountain roads and skiing on double-black-diamond slopes. I also enjoy less demanding but beautiful things like hiking in the mountains in fall, the ocean, a campfire, and music.

Then there are times when I've finished a class or come offstage from an improv performance or a concert, and it's almost like I don't even know where I've been. I've been so focused on what I'm doing and what's happening, so in "the zone," that I call it "becoming invisible."

Just as being in the moment can sound kind of unexciting, it can also sound kind of soft and ferny, like it's only a quality-of-life issue for type B hippies. While being in the moment can definitely improve your quality of life, I believe it also has very definite applications toward effectiveness, productivity, efficiency, and other hard, type A-sounding qualities.

Focusing on process means you're paying attention to what you need to do in order to be successful moment to moment. Be mindful and thorough. Use your technique. Don't half-ass it; full-ass it! Doing every step of a process well is the best way to achieve success. And if you don't succeed, it won't be because you didn't do your best.

Focusing on process doesn't mean you shouldn't have goals or plans. No, no, no, I'm a big fan of those things. But your plans and goals can blind you to opportunity if you let them. Focusing on process means that you're able to adapt if executing your plan isn't working. Get around the obstacle rather than just looking at it, wishing it weren't there.

Finally, focusing on process means you can be flexible enough to reach a satisfactory goal if your original goal becomes impossible or not worth the effort to reach. You might have been heading for point A, but point B and other points might still suffice—and they may even be better. My life has been full of this. I never set out to teach improv in a B-school, but I'm finding this to be more rewarding than so many of the other things I actually set out to do.

Exercises

Individual

1. Meditation is an ancient and respected way of getting into the moment. I'm not an expert in it, but there are many places, real and virtual, where you can study.

2. If sitting in a lotus position and staring at a candle while chanting "Om" (a gross stereotype of meditation) is not your style, there are other ways of getting into the moment, which I refer to as mindfulness exercises, Meditation Lite, or just chilling. Take exactly two minutes somewhere, perhaps outside if it's nice, and simply try to be aware of everything going on around you: sounds, sights, scents, and other sensations. When your mind starts to wander, gently coax it back into awareness of your surroundings. If you struggle, try it again another day. If it goes well, try adding time in 30-second increments. All you're trying to do here is be present in the moment.

3. If there are peak activities you enjoy, do them. Maybe it's something extreme or active. Maybe it's assembling jigsaw puzzles. Create time for whatever it is that consumes you. The more often you're in the moment, the easier it becomes to get into it, regardless of the situation.

4. Journaling can help (but sometimes doesn't). Specifically, if you find yourself distracted, note what is distracting you and explore those distractions. Perhaps by focusing energy on them, they'll stop demanding it from you.

Group

1. **Meal**

   A. Divide into groups of four to six and have each group think of three foods, and be sure that each member knows what the food is and how to eat it. Be specific; no one walks into an ice-cream shop and says, "I'd like some ice cream." Instead, we specify flavors, cup or cone, toppings, and so on.

   B. Each group takes a turn eating their foods in front of the rest of the participants. They don't have to purchase, prepare, raise, or slaughter the meal, only eat it. Direct the players to focus on the imaginary sensations. After 90 seconds or so, stop the players and have the audience guess what they're eating.

   C. When you see players looking at the audience or the teacher/director, gently suggest that they focus on eating the food. They're looking for approval when they should be looking at what they're doing. Seeking approval is human nature, but blatantly seeking it makes it harder to earn. People who are engaged in what they're doing are engaging to watch. They convey confidence and authority.

   D. Encourage the players to be deliberate and to take their time. If the audience doesn't guess the foods correctly, it doesn't mean the performers did poorly. Likewise, the audience might guess the foods right, but the performers didn't do well. The goal is to eat the imaginary food. You and your group might find that you lose interest in the somewhat shallow guessing aspect of the exercise and become more interested in simply observing the players eat and what evolves from that.

E. More than anything else, pay attention to the players. Ask them how they're doing. It's much better to have an unplanned discussion rather than imposing some canned coaching. The players might have a better idea of why they're struggling or succeeding than you do. They might find the exercise awkward because it is if only because it's not something we normally do. Again, suggest that they focus on the task at hand rather than their discomfort; that's the best way I know to get through awkwardness.

F. For distance learning, simply put your subgroups into breakout rooms to plan. When you bring them back to the main room, have the groups take turns performing by leaving their video on while the audience turns off their cameras.

2. **Celebrity Press Conference**

A. Ask for a volunteer. Explain that they will leave the room and upon returning be someone famous (living or dead, any gender, fictitious or real). While the volunteer is out of the room, the audience decides the volunteer's celebrity identity. The volunteer returns and the audience asks questions, which the volunteer must answer. Embedded within the questions are clues to the volunteer's identity. The questions should start obscure and then become more obvious. When the volunteer thinks they know who they are, they say the famous person's name while answering a question. If the answer is correct, the audience applauds and the game is done. If the answer is wrong, the audience is silent and the game continues. If the game goes on for more than 20 questions, be merciful and ask some easy questions with really obvious hints to end it.

B. At the end of the game, ask the volunteer to assess their performance. Then ask the audience to assess it. Most of the time the audience will have a much more favorable opinion than the player will. I feel you cannot point out this phenomenon too often. It demonstrates not only that our self-evaluation is usually negative but that it's also usually inaccurate.

    C. If the volunteer struggles, that is a teaching moment. Do whatever you can to support and encourage that person so they don't become disheartened. If the player struggles, you'll probably notice a change in body language. Mention it and give specific notes ("You shrank," "You were giving yourself a hug," etc.). I touch on it elsewhere in this book, but, essentially, once you start behaving like a loser, you're going to lose.

    D. You might notice that the longer the volunteer takes to solve the mystery, the more desperate they get. They want to solve the problem and end the game. They keep telling themselves and sometimes even the audience, verbally or physically, that they have no idea who they are. These inner voices can become so loud that the volunteers stop paying close attention to the questions/hints. (How do I know? I've experienced it firsthand [physician, heal thyself!] and observed it many times.) This is a prime example of not being in the moment and being too focused on the goal. The players seek so hard that they stop *seeing*. I coach the players to keep answering the questions and try to stay cool and trust that the answer will eventually come to them. And even if it doesn't, which is rare, there's really nothing at stake. Their pride might be wounded, but you can celebrate that they were brave enough to volunteer when others did not.

    E. This game adapts well to virtual environments. Instead of sending the volunteer out of the actual room, you send them to a breakout room. I like to send an escort with them, in real life and virtually. This gives them company and also gives you a control of sorts; the escort's perception of the game and processing of the mystery might differ from the volunteer's because the escort doesn't feel any pressure.

3. **Patterns**

    A. In Patterns, six to 12 people stand in a circle. The leader starts and ends each pattern. There are three patterns (but don't mention that at the start): one in which you point to someone and say "You," two in which you point to someone different and say their name, and three in which you point to someone else and say your name. Just as the leader points to someone, that second person points to a third and so on until the pattern winds up back at the leader. Each pattern should be different (i.e., players point to different players in different patterns).

B. Practice each pattern on its own after it's created until the group does it smoothly.

C. After the first two patterns are established, try having both going at the same time.

D. Once the third pattern is created, try having all three patterns going at the same time. It will be hard, and you might not succeed.

E. As you start with multiple patterns and players start to struggle, instruct them to stay focused on the moment. When they start thinking about a mistake they just made, they're walking right into another mistake. When they think about how hard it's going to be, they're getting distracted and psyching themselves out.

F. Point out that the game is essentially simple: responding correctly to three different stimuli. Also remind the players that there are really no consequences for failure. Reminding oneself of stakes can help diminish stress.

G. Having players point as they advance the pattern helps; remember it is a *team* exercise, so players have to look after each other. You haven't advanced the pattern if you point and speak, but the other player doesn't perceive and advance the pattern further. Players might have to repeat themselves or do something else to get another player's attention.

H. Due to lag, the lack of spatial connection, and the need for simultaneous sound, I don't think you could play this game online.

4. **Predator/Defender**

A. Each player secretly chooses a predator and a defender, whom they must keep between themself and the predator when the leader says "go."

B. Say "go." This game is bedlam and can resolve in many different ways: a line of people, a swirling mass, a pulsating blob.

C. Play it twice, and note how the versions differ.
D. The point is that we do not operate in a vacuum. Your actions affect others, and their actions and reactions affect you. Don't delude yourself into believing that your plans will go as expected because once you start to implement them, they and you will be altered by those affected by the plan. This is a demonstration of why one must be aware of and react to what's really happening rather than focusing on expectations or desires, which are not real, no matter how strongly we sense them. (Sorry, I don't know of a way to play Predator/Defender in a virtual environment.)

7

Leading by Following

"Follow the follower."—Paul Sills

Leadership in improv is tricky and hard to define. The nature of making things up on the fly requires an improviser to support the initiations of other players and also to make their own initiations clear enough to be followed and supported. Players must be ready to see their initiations altered or abandoned entirely. Individual control is impossible in improv—at least in good improv.

Most improvisers want to be funny and to make people laugh with their wit and creativity, and that's perfectly understandable. However, as I've stated earlier in this book, improv is only partially about the individual improviser. More important is the collaboration among players. Improvisers must learn to listen to and watch their partners and care about what they're saying and doing. That sounds a lot like following, doesn't it?

Of course, if all players are following each other, then they're inherently and oxymoronically leading. The interrelationship between following and leading is hard to define precisely, but that's where improv's magic happens and good improvisers learn to trust it.

Who's in charge isn't important in improv; that the players are connected and moving each other forward is. This model of leadership (or followership) has a lot to teach us in nontheatrical settings.

Our society is obsessed with leadership, and if you haven't taken a leadership course or workshop, you've certainly heard of them. "We develop leaders." "Tell us about a time you exhibited leadership." "Take me to your leader."

We don't talk about following as much. For one thing, it just doesn't sound sexy, and it hasn't for a very long time. As long as people have been telling stories, we've focused on the leaders rather than the followers, so it's only natural that we should become obsessed with leaders and leadership. But being a leader isn't automatically a positive thing; you've got to be a *good* leader.

Perhaps we're taught leadership poorly, maybe even starting with our earliest childhood experiences. When we're young, we're often dictated to and have no say in what we do. This is largely necessary until we develop the judgment to make our own decisions, but, regardless, I believe it creates an early thirst for power.

As children we even play games in which we vie to be the leader and tyrannize our playmates. Follow the Leader and Simon Says are simple and fun, but if you start psychoanalyzing them, they start to seem a little scary. The leader wins, and the follower loses if the leader can get the follower to make a mistake.

In our early years at home, school, and elsewhere we learn that there are serious consequences to challenging leadership. We might get sent to our rooms or the principal's office for sassing or rebelling. Often this fearful reverence for leadership continues throughout our lives or morphs into a knee-jerk reaction against it. In short, most of us have some baggage regarding leadership, and, if you're a leader, you quickly become aware of how true that is. Leaders often receive punches intended for someone else at some other time.

Once we get into the position of leadership, we face a whole new set of challenges, both from without and within. We might not have had good leaders or healthy leadership dynamics to emulate, so we revert to the only examples we've known. We can also feel insecure as leaders, which is natural if you're new to a specific leadership role. If you're new to leadership in general, that insecurity is exacerbated.

I suspect that when most of us first become a leader, we think, "Oh goodie, now I get to call the shots and control what happens." But—surprise!—you never get to control what happens, and often you don't even get to call the shots because you're limited by circumstances and your followers. Moreover, you have to earn the respect of your followers and endure the challenges they pose to you, the same challenges you posed to other leaders.

While different individuals and cultures benefit from differing leaders and leadership approaches, leading and following are often depicted as binary. Put another way, it too frequently seems we follow stupid jerks and lead incompetent slobs.

Improv's "follow the follower" approach offers an alternative. I first heard the term used by Paul Sills and interpret it to mean that the leader is dedicated to the team and all its members, including himself or herself, and the team's task. The followers are likewise dedicated. All are empowered and responsible for the performance of the team and its members. (This might sound a little like *kaizen*, the process of continuous improvement developed by Japanese manufacturers and businesses, most notably Toyota, after World War II.)[8]

If one member is failing, it concerns everyone, and all should try to remedy the situation. It happens that some team members cannot fit into a team, but blaming struggling members for their failures and flaws should not be the first reaction of the team. Instead, the team should try to figure out how to help the member—and thus the team—succeed.

That's all nice and ethereal, so maybe a physical activity can help demonstrate the "follow the follower" concept and its value, in both the improv and the "real" worlds.

Mirroring is a simple, playful exercise with profound potential takeaways. Aside from mirroring while playing as a little kid, I remember mirroring exercises from my first theater classes in elementary school. Later I experienced them again in improv workshops.

Participants pair up, with one being A and the other B. The goal is for each pair to move together as one. Start by having A lead B. B does everything A does, only in reverse (i.e., B moves the right arm when A moves the left). This is a nonspeaking exercise, although laughing, sneezing, farting, and so on are perfectly acceptable as long as they are mirrored or, more accurately, echoed.

As with Gesture Circle discussed earlier, movements in this exercise should be random, unfamiliar, abstract, and meaningless as opposed to mime, specific expressive gestures, dance moves, yoga, tai chi, or anything of that nature. The players should mirror what they *see*, not the *idea* that they think they see. If they think their partner is brushing their teeth or doing the Macarena, they will do that movement, but they'll almost certainly stop mirroring the actual physicality.

If you're facilitating this exercise, you're likely to see a wide variety of things, and some of it will actually be mirroring. Some pairs will get the idea right away and might be so in synch that you can't be sure who's leading.

In other pairs you'll see A deliberately trying to lose B, turning the exercise into a contest. In some pairs A will be far ahead of B or doing something entirely different because there's a lack of attention on the part of either or both players. You might see A doing extremely complex or fast movements that B simply cannot mirror simultaneously. Sometimes you'll see A turn in profile to B, which makes things very tough for B. Sometimes you'll even see A turn their *back* on B, which makes things pretty much impossible for B.

Often you'll see players clearly feeling awkward with mirroring. When you pause after the first iteration of the exercise, it's good to ask participants how they're doing and acknowledge that mirroring is kind of intimate and intense or at least outside of their regular routines. Hey, improvisers, actors, and dancers do this crap all the time, but some of the participants might not have ever done it at all.

While your group is paused, ask if they're achieving the goal of the exercise (to move together as one). What challenges are they facing?

Some players might say it's hard to think of things to do as the leader, particularly "creative" things. Ask them why they think they need to be creative in this exercise. Are they trying to entertain their partner? Why? Being creative or entertaining is not the goal of the game, moving together is. While that drive or need to be "good" isn't inherently bad, it's an example of mission creep and the stress we sometimes needlessly put on ourselves.

Tell your players what you've observed. Compliment the people who did especially well. Mention the difficulty some pairs had, perhaps without mentioning them specifically. Ask them how they can tell when they're moving together. (Answer: The leader looks.) You might mention that the mirror leader is in charge of getting their team to achieve its goal of moving in unison. The leader might have all sorts of ideas of what they want to do, but, if their partner isn't doing them, then the team is failing.

Have the Bs take a turn leading. Suggest they apply as the leader what they learned as the follower.

Good leaders are followable. This is the primary takeaway of this exercise. Mirroring illustrates the basics of good leadership in the simplest way, and yet people who self-identify as leaders often miss them.

As a leader you must first establish a connection with your team. Start slowly. Then, as you notice they're following you and trust is developing, you can speed up and make things more challenging. But when you've lost your followers, you must slow down and reconnect with them.

In processing this exercise with your group, solicit and offer relevant examples of good and bad leadership.

I can certainly think of many times when I could have been a better leader. One very good (or bad) and simple example was a time when Transactors Improv was playing a theater in Charleston, South Carolina. The drive was five hours, and, by the time we arrived, my mind was on a lot of things, mostly what we had to do to be prepared for the evening's show.

When I parked the van, I got out and went straight to the stage door. To my surprise, when I reached it, I discovered I was alone. *Where are those lousy followers of mine*, I thought, or something to that effect, only less savory. I went back to the van, fuming slightly. "What are you guys doing?" I asked my colleagues.

"Well, we were wondering where you went," replied one.

Instantly I realized that the problem wasn't with the followers but with the leader. Had I expected them to read my mind? I should have told them where I was going, maybe checked to see if they were ready to go.

Or I could've done even better by discussing the various things we needed to do and delegating the responsibility. I could talk to the presenter while others handled other tasks like reconnoitering the stage and green rooms, talking to the technical staff, making sure we had water, and so on.

I learned. I keep learning. I think I've progressed to the point as a leader that when I see a problem with the followers, my first question is whether or not I could have been more followable. Sometimes the problem's with me. Sometimes it's with the other person or people. Usually it's a combination of the two and can be resolved without great difficulty or hurt feelings.

There are other lessons from the mirroring game, lessons that are essential to developing as an improviser. They're not as clear-cut as the takeaway about being a followable leader, but they're important. First you need to play the game a little more though.

After everyone has had a chance to lead and to follow a couple times, I like to throw in a conundrum. Reiterating that the goal remains to move in unison and that there is no talking, I tell the teams that everyone should lead. That generally results in laughter, which is a good thing, and some bemused looks, which is okay too. After some tentative beginnings, most players get more spirited in their play.

"Now focus on playing and doing the exercise *well* instead of doing it right," I'll instruct. "Be bold. Have fun." Things start getting pretty wild. It can look like a dance party. Sometimes pairs will even pair up, and you'll have four or more people, all leading and yet all moving together somehow.

"Now, everyone, follow." This instruction is a relative buzzkill. Most everyone stands still, remembers to feel awkward, and steals glances at me, hoping I'll end this impossible exercise and with it their misery.

Some players find a way to continue the game though. To make it easier on those who are stuck I'll suggest that they mirror every little thing their partner is doing, intentionally or not. Maybe their partners are grinning or shuffling. Certainly they're breathing. There's *something* to mirror. You might think that someone *isn't* moving because they're not *supposed* to be moving (or at least not initiating movement), and yet that person might be fidgeting or flirting or something else. If the players can mirror these smaller, unintentional movements, everyone following becomes a funhouse as each mirroring is mirrored.

Finally, with everyone still in following mode, I'll suggest the players exaggerate what their partners are doing. "If they twitch, you jerk. If they jerk, you jump." (It can start to sound like Sean Connery's "The Chicago Way" monologue in *The Untouchables*.) This leads to quick exaggeration of exaggerations and then bedlam, at which point I'll stop the exercise. By this point players are usually laughing again, a good thing.

When we process the various versions of the mirroring game, most people like best the part when everyone's leading. It feels freer, they say. I'll ask how they managed it, and most report that they tacitly traded leadership roles based on intuition. This is the relationship at the heart of improvising with other people and creating chemistry with partners. We're playing off each other. No one's in control, but all participants bear responsibility for what's happening. Creativity flourishes with this highly democratic arrangement.

Hierarchy has its place. However, in improv and collaborative creation, having everyone simultaneously leading and following, or perhaps taking informal turns leading as in a relay race, can take you to amazing, unexpected places. Insisting on rigid rather than liquid leadership roles quashes creativity.

In improv we're looking to find something new, something outside of our conscious egos. We want to get lost, surrender our need to control, and discover something that we couldn't have found on our own. We need that unexpected input and response from someone else to take us out of the familiar and to the transcendent.

From the very start of my improv career, I was good at the art form. Or at least I received positive responses from audiences because I was a talented and energetic actor with a quick wit. But maybe I wasn't actually that good at improv.

You see, my unstated approach was that I would go along with someone else's idea in a scene if they would follow my leadership in another. That's fair, but it's also very limiting because it revolves around one person being in control and having an idea, *knowing* what they're doing.

My first quantum leap in improv was letting go of the need to control or be controlled. If I could respond to my partner and vice versa and then we each start responding to our responses to each other, we can escape the known and go somewhere that neither of us could envision on our own.

When I stopped trying to do it all by myself and started working with others and letting them help me, I improved. Whereas I had once been talented with ad-libs, I became a true improviser who could contribute to a group's success.

My ego, which craved recognition, was still gratified by the success of the group. I was being less self-centered but still getting my strokes. My ego might've even been gratified by being less egoistic. Sublimating the ego doesn't mean destroying or forgetting about it; it means setting the ego aside, escaping from it for a while. Remember: we're inherently self-interested animals, so we need to see the potential personal reward, the cookie for the ego.

Once you've introduced the concept of mirroring in improv, you'll find it comes back a lot. Mirroring onstage can get you moving in the right direction if you're stuck. Don't know what to do? Do what your scene partner is doing! You might still be stuck, but at least you'll be connected to your partner, which is your best hope for getting unstuck.

Offstage it's not quite that simple, but an aspect of mirroring that I've found helpful is to increase your awareness of and connection to others—as if you were going to mirror them in this exercise—when you don't know what to do or say. For example, soliciting questions or feedback in a presentation or meeting can get you back on track if you're off it. Instead of floundering alone, you can create dialogue with your audience. You might not be going where you thought you were going to go, but you're going somewhere and you're going there together.

Another thing to keep in mind is that mirroring is natural and inherently intimate. You don't have to look far to see people mirroring each other unconsciously. Savvy negotiators know the power of mirroring and how it can create an atmosphere of goodwill and trust.[9] Sometimes a lack of mirroring can indicate conflict.

Respond to the people and the world around you rather than solely what's in your head. You might be surprised by what you discover and the changes you see in that person in the mirror.

Exercises

Individual

1. Think of the best leaders you've been around (parents, teachers, coaches, bosses, etc.), and think about the ways they led. What made you like their leadership?
2. Think of times you succeeded and failed as a leader. How do they differ? How are they similar? Perhaps circumstances changed your approach, or perhaps different situations called for different approaches.
3. Think of the worst followers you've had. Could you have handled them better? Maybe you could have ceded some control and followed them a little.
4. Notice times when you find yourself mirroring other people without thinking about it.
5. Notice little things that other people are doing around you as though you had to mirror them. You don't have to mirror them but pay attention. What does their behavior seem to communicate?
6. Practice mirroring other people. Do it subtly (i.e., don't stand next to your spouse pretending to brush your teeth when they're brushing). See if it affects you, the other person, or the situation. If you have a mild conflict with someone, try

mirroring that person and see if it has an effect (do not try this in a bar fight).

Group

Mirroring

1. Divide the group into twos, and have each pair label themselves A and B. If you have an uneven number, you can have a trio of A, B, and C, which creates some different opportunities and challenges from working in a pair but is essentially the same exercise. Emphasize that the goal throughout the exercise is always to move in unison and also that there should be no talking. Move now, talk later; talking is often a way of camouflaging discomfort.
2. A leads and B follows. If you're coaching this exercise, politely help the pairs as they play. You might ask the leader to slow down, to be more deliberate, or just to think about B.
3. B leads and A follows.
4. Pause and discuss challenges and successes teams and individuals are having in the exercise.
5. Repeat steps 2 and 3 without stopping between steps. (If your group has a team of three, be sure to give C a chance to lead.)
6. Again, without stopping, instruct everyone to lead. Instruct the players to be bold and playful and not worry about making mistakes. Suggest they do it *well*, not *right*.
7. Transition directly to everyone following. Encourage the players to mirror every little thing their partner is doing, even unintentional things. Then have them exaggerate what their partner is doing.
8. Process the exercise. What did people experience, observe, think, and feel? What are the takeaways? Be open to some takeaways you didn't expect.

8

Creativity

What Is It and Who Has It?

"Creativity comes from trust. Trust your instincts. And never hope more than you work."—Rita Mae Brown

Creativity and innovation were the big buzzwords at the MBA Leadership Conference presented by the Graduate Management Admission Council some years ago in Newport Beach, California. Businesses want creativity and innovation in order to win and maintain competitive advantages. Business schools want to turn out graduates versed in these skills.

So in typical business and academic fashion we set out to quantify those things. There's nothing wrong with that, and I was waiting in line to steal whatever statistics we could find. But honestly, I just don't know how accurate or useful measures or even definitions of creativity and innovation are.

I do know that creativity is more a process than a quality. It's highly inefficient and requires commitment, patience, and a sense of play to use. And this is true if you're an improviser, a businessperson, a musician, or an architect. More than anything else, creativity requires *doing*. I don't believe there are "creative" and "uncreative" people, just people who create and people who don't.

Jeff DeGraff, Clinical Professor of Management and Organizations at the University of Michigan Ross Business School, presented at that GMAC conference and referred to a fascinating study. A group of ceramics artists was instructed to create (1) an "ideal" or "perfect" piece and (2) 100 pieces while focusing purely on quantity rather than quality. Judges rated each artist's work, and in each case the piece selected as "best" was not one the artist intended as best but one that came from the lot of 100. DeGraff's sensible conclusion is that where creativity is concerned, "Quantity is quality."

Twice, shortly after that conference, I happened to find myself talking to piano players who didn't consider themselves creative. They're adept at playing, they both said, but when it came to improvising, they were terrible. "Who told you that you were terrible?" I asked each player. Both admitted that was their own opinion, which in my mind, isn't that valuable. It's a part of that phenomenon that makes us hate the sound of our own voices when they're recorded.

"How much time did you spend practicing your piano improvisation?" I then asked. Each player responded that they devoted very little time to that skill, so it was no surprise they didn't master improvisation when they didn't work at it. One was heartbroken she didn't sound like jazz great Bill Evans, but he certainly worked for years developing his craft. If she had done the same, she might have developed a style that equaled his. Or maybe not, but she certainly would have improved.

When people tell me I'm a fine improviser, I tend to reply, "Thanks, but after doing this for so long, it would be a shame if I weren't." Yes, I feel I have some native talent, but it's the work that's made me excel. By comparison, few who have seen my rare drawings would say I'm a great artist, but then I've spent almost no time on that since I was a kid.

Practice makes perfect? I don't think so. But practice is the only way you'll get good. "Practice makes permanent," I'm told they say in the U.S. Marine Corps. Striving for perfection, as DeGraff's example suggests, isn't really relevant.

Practice—*doing*—is commitment.

Commitment means that you're sticking around for the bad stuff. Staying around for the good stuff, whether it's in a relationship, a job, or trying to be more creative, is a no-brainer. But commitment means you'll stay with it through the fights, the small bonuses, and the poems you really hate.

Committing to creativity and innovation means you're willing to accept that you might not wind up where you want to go. It means a lot of work might wind up at a dead end. The only promise is that the more you work at creativity, the better you get at the process and the more likely it is that you'll create something wonderful. Create your 100 pieces, and trust that something tremendous will be among them.

If you don't consider yourself an artist, you might well be wondering what creativity has to do with you anyway. The way I see it, creativity is a big umbrella, and underneath that umbrella are things like artistry, innovation, adaptation, problem-solving, and organization. Some of these things sound pretty sexy, and some don't.

For example, how exciting is organization? Maybe it is and maybe it's not, but, the fact is that if you're good at organizing things, you have the creative talent of seeing order and patterns where other people see only chaos, just as a sculptor might look at a block of marble and see a figure where others see only rock.

I'd like to reiterate that creativity is highly valued in the business world. "According to a major IBM survey of more than 1,500 Chief Executive Officers from 60 countries and 33 industries worldwide, chief executives believe that—more than rigor, management discipline, integrity, or even vision—successfully navigating an increasing[ly] complex world will require creativity."[10] The creativity these CEOs cite applies to everyday people and not just folks like composers and dancers.

Now whether or not business really wants creativity or knows how to foster it is debatable. However, there's no denying that business thinks and says it wants creativity. So it behooves you to identify ways in which you're creative and be able to promote them. This might sound like mere hype, but I truly believe we can all benefit by recognizing our various talents. If they appeal to others as well, then so much the better. Once you've identified your creative talents, you might want to develop them further.

One of the problems nonartists—and even some artists—face is that they don't *think* of themselves as creative, and this becomes a self-fulfilling prophesy. When we start to address creativity in my business classes, I like to take an informal poll and ask who considers themselves to be creative. Usually fewer than 20 percent of students raise a hand, and some of them do so tentatively.

I ask those who didn't raise their hands why they don't consider themselves creative. Usually I'll hear a response like, "My second-grade teacher told me I couldn't draw," or, "My high school friends made fun of my singing."

My response to this is twofold. First, don't confuse artistry with creativity. Second, isn't it amazing how an offhand comment can haunt us throughout our lives, especially when it's about something as sensitive and deep-seated as our creativity? So many people have told me about creativity trauma they've suffered; something negative said by a teacher, parent, or friend has stuck with and defined them for decades. If you've experienced something like that, I encourage you to put it behind you and redefine yourself according to your own terms. Your opinion matters.

I also like to ask people who identify as noncreative what their skills are. Pretty much every skill they mention relates back to creativity. "I can manage people." That's using imagination in the form of empathy to understand and connect with those being led. "I can diagnose budget issues and suggest solutions." That's problem-solving. "I'm a really good baker." Well, baking is certainly creating something, and any baker can tell you there are almost always unexpected problems that must be solved quickly.

We are inherently creative animals. We build things: homes, families, societies, languages, legacies, bodies of work, history, world records, etc., etc. To deny your creativity is to deny a part of your humanity. Finding your creativity is liberating, empowering, and ennobling.

"Creativity … is much romanticized," psychotherapist Thomas Moore writes in his book, *Care of the Soul*. We invest it "with idealism and lofty fantasies of exceptional achievement. In this sense, most work is not creative. It is ordinary, repetitious, and democratic.

"But if we were to bring our very idea of creativity down to earth it would not have to be reserved for exceptional individuals or identified with brilliance. In ordinary life creativity means making something for the soul out of every experience."[11]

So don't just sit there; *do* something. You will find your creativity.

Exercises

Individual

1. Solo Sevens is similar to the group version of Sevens described in Chapter 2. Think of a category; pretty much anything will do: animals, breakfast cereals, types of shoes, prostheses…. As fast as you can, say seven things that belong in that category. And it doesn't matter whether or not your answer is made up. We're looking for quantity and speed here, not quality. It's just an exercise to help improve your mind's agility and get your judging brain to shut up for a while.

2. It requires commitment and effort, but *The Artist's Way*[12] is an outstanding book/course designed to help you reclaim your artistic self. Author Julia Cameron asserts that all of us have an artistic urge and sense but that we often lose it because of emotional injury or neglect. Even if you are an active artist, this course can be very enlightening and helpful.
3. Make a list of your talents. Explore how these skills relate to creativity. The list does not have to include artistic endeavors. Pick one talent, and find a way to use it. Maybe you can try preparing a new dish or repairing something around the house. Maybe there's a volunteer opportunity where you can use your people skills. Start small, and don't overwhelm yourself.
4. If your skills are artistic, that's fine too! Paint, act, sing karaoke. Take a dance class. You have no one to answer to but yourself. People are often cruel to others and to themselves as well. If you hear cruel criticism of your efforts, remind yourself (or that critic) that you're trying to develop and that you know you have some way to go. Everyone has to start somewhere.

Group

1. **Sevens**
   This exercise is described and recommended for distance learning in Chapter 2. However, it's a great in-person exercise too.
2. **Paired Drawing**
   Not to be confused with Impaired Drawing, players work in teams of two. This is a nonspeaking exercise.
   A. Each team should have several pieces of paper, and each player should have a pen or pencil.
   B. Players take turns drawing parts of a face. Perhaps Player 1 draws an eye, and Player 2 draws an eyebrow. Or maybe Player 2 draws a chin or hair or whatever.
   C. When the players feel they are done with a face, they name it, one letter at a time.
   D. Each team should do two to three faces. Then all the teams lay the faces they've drawn on the floor, and the entire group looks at the exhibition.

3. **Free Association**
    A. One player starts by saying a word, the next player responds with the first word that comes to mind, then the next player responds, and so on. There are no right or wrong words; that's what the "free" in free association means.
    B. If you have international players, invite them to respond in whatever language first comes to mind. Why? Because the words are stimuli and not necessarily data. If someone says a word in Mandarin or Portuguese, I might not understand the word, but it will still provoke *some* response in my brain, and I must be aware of that response.
    C. Play the game for a few minutes, and then stop to see how it's going for your group. Discuss challenges, and see if there are ways to make the exercise less stressful and more rewarding.
    D. Play the game again to see if there are any changes. You might suggest players sit in a "ready" position or close their eyes and see if such adjustments make a difference.
    E. The goal is for each player to become aware of their first response to stimulus. This response is generated by who you are, ranging from your genetic makeup to the culture in which you live, and is the root of your innate and unique creativity. Listen to those immediate responses; they are the seeds of your creativity. You don't have to act on all your impulses, but you should be aware of them.

9

Yes and There Is
a Chapter on "Yes-And"

"Hell is other people."—Jean-Paul Sartre

Collaboration can be hard as hell. If only there weren't those other people around to mess up your great ideas. If only those other people would be responsible, see things your way, and put you in charge. Most of us have felt that way when working with others, and many times there are good reasons for it. But for as much as collaboration challenges us, it also offers a great deal of potential. Perhaps most importantly, working with other people can get us to a place we can't reach on our own.

Improv is a great illustrator of this. By definition (mine, at least) a group activity, improv demands that you pay attention to your partners and support them. Accept that, and you start to understand that finding something new—innovating—requires you to lose control of the process and let go of the known. By responding to your partner and your partner's reacting to you, you both find yourselves in an unfamiliar place, somewhere you couldn't have planned to go, and this is the mysterious gateway to collaborative creation.

Saying yes is essentially the opposite of maintaining control. And, oh, do we want control! "No" might not be the first word a child uses, but it certainly gets a lot of use during that period of early development known as the "terrible twos." The child, previously helpless and powerless, is attempting to establish some power and self-determination. It might not be able to do or express all the things that an adult can, but it can refuse to do them. It's not much power nor is it much control, but it's *something.*

Almost all of us go through this as infants, and a lot of us never

71

get that far away from it. No represents security and invulnerability in a world full of unknowns. No and the need to control become habitual. So the most well-known and often most profound lesson for beginning improvisers is learning to say yes.

"Yes-And" is a phrase so commonly used in teaching and directing improv that it's actually become rather well known, even to the point of ridicule. Of the many improv books I've read every single one mentions "yes and." Yet there is a reason for its frequent usage, and, really, nothing else will quite do the job. To avoid discussing "yes and" because other improv books mention it would be like skipping Beethoven just because other books on classical music mention him. Just as "yes" unlocks one's potential, "yes and" is the heart of cooperation.

"Yes-And" means listening and building. It means accepting the offers that others have been kind enough to extend to you. Here's how it might look on an improv stage:

"It's raining."

"Yes and I will share my umbrella with you."

Or....

"Grampa, you're drunk!"

"Yes and I want to find that bayonet I brought back from Korea."

The flip side of "yes and" is called denial, meaning you're refusing your partner's offer and thus stymying their idea and thus the scene. With denial we have:

"It's raining."

"No, it's not."

Or....

"Grampa, you're drunk."

"No, I'm the ghost of St. Francis of Assisi, and I've taken a vow of celibacy and therefore could not have offspring. Also, I took a vow of sobriety and am drinking tea. What are you doing here, talking alpaca?"

It's easy to see how progress in a scene can come to a halt when partners don't agree and work together in the same direction. You might not like the first step, but ignoring or trying to undo it creates an even bigger problem.

As it is in improv, so it is in the real world. "Yes-And" is especially useful early in creative processes, a prime example being brainstorming. When you're trying to innovate, you need new ideas and new combinations of them—if you didn't, you would have already thought of the innovation.

So you must welcome all input, even if it strikes you as bad and sometimes *especially* if it strikes you as bad. I've seen amazing things develop when people can table the need to be good for a while. If a group is stuck in a creative or adaptive process, I might instruct them to try to think of the worst possible ideas. Sometimes combining two bad ideas can make one good idea. If a speaker is struggling, I might direct them to be as bad as possible. It's counterintuitive, but when you stop evaluating every little thing you're doing, you have more energy to invest in *doing* it, and that can lead to astounding results.

At the start of a process, you're looking for potential, and therefore you want all the grist you can find for your creative mill. The bad ideas and the ones that don't fit have a way of falling away on their own. And when they don't, that's when refinement and editing take place, toward the end of the process and not at the beginning.

Creative collaboration, regardless of the setting, requires getting at least a little bit lost. That's where the discovery happens, and it's the only way to find something new. You have to view your colleagues as necessary partners on your expedition, not as adversaries who are keeping you from having your way. You have to find safety in mutual trust with your partners rather than in your familiar old ideas.

And speaking of the personal aspect of "yes and," you risk alienating team members if you start denigrating or refusing their suggestions when you should simply be accepting them. They might check out and start playing with their phone, in which case you might lose potentially valuable contributions. They might also get angry and decide to retaliate by negating your or others' suggestions. Then you have destruction on your hands instead of construction.

Avoiding denial was one of our central tenets when I first started with Transactors Improv. Even though I was the novice in the group, we were all pretty new to improv and feeling our way along, trying to reconcile our own experiences with the instruction we'd received from various teachers. That instruction often focused on the necessity of agreement.

Yet in rehearsal one night we had a scene that went well despite one of the players' saying no in it. We debated at length about whether or not this was denial and, if so, if denial was always a bad thing. Company member Dan Sipp suggested the deceptively simple concept that denial between *characters* wasn't bad but that denial between *players* was. In other words, as long as the actors agree, the characters can disagree.

Taking that a step further, we discovered that, as crazy as it sounds, if a character says yes to something they shouldn't say yes to, that can be denial. It can deny the character's truth or a scene's premise. So you can say yes to something and actually be guilty of denial in improv. Perhaps that could be called "over-affirmation."

It's worth noting that, while some people feel conflict is a requirement in scripted theater, I don't feel overt conflict is necessary for good improv scenes. Even if characters agree on everything, dramatic tension arises because of the omnipresent possibility of conflict. Conflict can arise or, maybe even more interestingly, fail to arise. Regardless, conflict isn't something you have to push in improv. For beginners it's important to instill the "yes and" mindset. For more experienced players who seem determined to find conflict, suggest that they relax, follow the flow of interactions and scenes, and be open to the possibility of agreement between characters.

As I mentioned in the chapter on leadership, when I first began improvising, my approach was that I'd go along with someone else's idea in a scene if they'd go along with mine later. While that's fair, it's also tremendously limiting. When I could cede control and the need to know where I was and where we were going, the payoff was excitement, mystery, and exponentially increased creative potential. Instead of unwritten skits and ego-limited ad-libs, I was performing *improvised scenes* with other people. This daunting passage required trust in others and the process.

The possibility of being amazing requires the risk of failure, which is not that big a deal in improv because the stakes are rarely very high. Failure can have greater consequences in the real world, but, then again, not being amazing can have great consequences too.

The implications of "yes and" go far beyond improv and collaborative processes on or off the stage.

If we can gain a little detachment and see ourselves as Shakespeare described us, as players on the stage that is the world, we might be able to resolve conflicts a little more easily. Specifically, rather than denying an opposing view, we might say, "Yes and we can find some common ground and perhaps a mutually acceptable solution."

I feel that most of us are far too ready to dig in our heels and defend our position in conflict rather than accept that compromise is possible. If we can agree on our common humanity and a goal of a mutually acceptable resolution, we can more easily accept our differences so that it's like we're improvisers agreeing on a premise while playing characters who disagree. Call me a dreamer. (Shakespeare also wrote "Life is but a dream.")

If you're in conflict with someone, it's not helpful to say, "There's no problem here." That's denial just like in an improv scene. You cannot solve a problem unless you acknowledge it. If your partner, be they professional, artistic, and/or romantic, says, "I have a problem," it's inherently a shared problem. The solution might be to dissolve the partnership, but up to that point it's a mutual issue.

At its heart, "yes and" is "radical acceptance," a term with roots in the work of psychologist Marsha Linehan.[13] Therapist Karyn Hall explains, "Accepting reality is difficult when life is painful. No one wants to experience pain, disappointment, sadness, or loss. But those experiences are a part of life. When you attempt to avoid or resist those emotions, you add suffering to your pain. You may build the emotion bigger with your thoughts or create more misery by attempting to avoid the painful emotions."[14] If that sounds a lot like the second arrow from Buddhism that I mentioned in the chapter on process, it should come as no surprise that psychologist Tara Brach connects the ideas in her book *Radical Acceptance: Embracing Your Life with the Heart of a Buddha.*[15]

"Yes-And" opens the door to possibility, creativity, and, as odd it as it sounds, both the imagination and reality.

Exercises

Individual

1. Watch the movie *Yes Man*. Hey, it's no *Citizen Kane*, but it's entertaining and its premise will have you asking questions about your own life. Alternately, you can watch *Groundhog Day* for the same reasons.

Group

1. **Yes-And Story**
   The group constructs a story one sentence at a time. I like to instruct my groups that our goal is to make sense, not to be good, funny, or clever, because our egos will often drive us to

show off and hurt the group effort. As a young improviser, I had to learn that a useful idea is better than a great one, and I think that also applies in real life.

    A. Start with your group in a circle and proceed in order around it. In a virtual environment, post a list of participants so that each knows whom they follow.

    B. The starter says a sentence.

    C. Each subsequent player adds a sentence that begins with "Yes-And."

    D. Continue as long as you like. For a group of 15 or more, once around is probably enough for starters. You might instruct the last person that their job is to finish the story.

    E. Ask the players how it went, what was challenging, and what was gratifying. They'll probably be able to diagnose their successes and shortcomings, the latter of which often includes inflexibility, not listening, and/or trying too hard. Gently offer your own observations.

    F. Ask the group why you had each player start with "Yes-And." Use the phrase "listen and build" if it doesn't arise organically in discussion.

    G. Ask the participants how they adapted or didn't adapt individually.

    H. Play the game a second time, and see if the group improves or regresses.

2. **One-Word-at-a-Time Story**

Virtually identical to Yes-And Story in its structure, One-Word-at-a-Time Story is much more difficult because players say only one word at a time rather than an entire sentence. It can be a lot of fun—and frustrating. You're likely to hear that players struggle because of their lack of control. Again, "funny" people can ruin a story that is on the verge of making sense because they want to force something great that just doesn't fit.

3. **Moving Picture** (I don't know that you can play this game in virtual environments because of its reliance on spatial relationships.)

    A. Ask a volunteer to think of a specific place and then, without speaking or any kind of introduction or explanation, begin an action appropriate to that place.

Emphasize that the volunteer thinks first of the place, not the action, and that the place should be specific. Specificity spurs creativity. Instruct the volunteer to take their time and be deliberate because that will help others to build off their movement.

B. Other participants join the moving picture one by one. They may be anything: people, animals, objects, natural phenomena. Regardless of what they do, they should look to accept and support the starter's idea. For example, if the starter is trimming a hedge, another player might see the offer as being the hedge, and another might become the hedge clippers. The starter might be thinking of a bowling alley, and others might add to the picture by being pins, the ball, the lane, the gutters, bowling partners, and so on.

C. Some participants will be hesitant to volunteer. If you're looking for a starter, tell them you'll come up with a place for their initial action (which you will whisper to them).

D. If players aren't joining the picture, ask them why. You're likely to hear that they're afraid of messing it up. That's fair enough, and I like to respond that if they can honestly say they're looking to support the starter that things will turn out okay. The picture might not turn out the way the starter thought, but at least there won't be dissension. There might be surprises, and there will definitely be changes. For example, the starter might think of a pool and lie down to tan on the deck. Someone watching might see that and think the starter is at a beach and add something appropriate for that locale but not a pool. That's okay. The place often isn't defined until a few or even several people have entered the picture. Surprises are welcome, but disagreement isn't.

E. Some participants might be hesitant to play because they say they can't think of what to add. Again, fair enough. But let's go back to the bowling alley example for a moment. If one person is a pin, then that's an offer for nine more. Or if there's one hedge being trimmed, there's usually another nearby. You might point out that participants are putting needless pressure on themselves to be original, and originality is not important in this exercise—playing is. I like to say in this exercise, "If the location seems to be indoors, you can always be a wall. If it's outside, you can be a tree." It just doesn't have to be that hard.

F. Play the game at least three times. If some people aren't getting involved, keep encouraging them. You might say, "Okay, this is the last picture, so I want to make sure that everyone gets the chance to be involved." Participation is potentially the principal learning in this and every exercise.

4. **Squirrel, Nut, Tree**

A. Form a circle. One person enters the center, poses like a squirrel, and says, "I'm a squirrel." Another person enters, poses like a tree, and says, "I'm a tree." And a third person enters, poses like a nut, and says, "I'm a nut."

B. The squirrel says, "Keep the tree" or "Keep the nut," indicating that one of the other two players remains in the center and will start the next montage. The other two players return to the circle. The one remaining in the middle keeps the posture and reiterates, "I'm a tree" or "I'm a nut." This is an offer for someone to add to the picture and create a new combination of three. Maybe someone joins the tree, saying, "I'm a swing," and a third comes in as a girl. Maybe the nut is joined by a bag and an elephant.

C. If you're in a virtual environment, the process is the same except that, of course, players can't step into the middle. Instead, they jump in with their physicality and their statement of what they are (and I encourage the physicality so that it's more than just a word game). I recommend breakout rooms of five or so to create lots of opportunity with little pressure.

D. Whoever stayed in picture two tells one of the new additions to stay, and the process is repeated. Ideally you go far, far away from the squirrel, the nut, and the tree. Maybe you even return to them. Maybe you start to explore smells, sounds, or ethereal things like

thoughts or desires. Some people like to end the game
by getting back to the starting montage, but others like
an open ending.

E. Get everyone involved! You might have to encourage
some people or even nudge them into a picture, telling
them what they are.

F. Try to keep the pace high. Avoid overcooking ideas; the
montages are here and gone in an instant and not worth
agonizing over.

G. Discuss how far the group progressed in the exercise.
Talk about what was fun, what was unexpected, and
the lack of control. This exercise is just one "yes and"
after another. Incidentally, I recommend this exercise
for groups that have some familiarity with each other
rather than those that are brand new.

10

Thinking Inside the Box

"Creativity requires the courage to let go of certainties."
—Erich Fromm

Most of us have heard and are probably sick of that rather threadbare cliché, "thinking outside the box." When people say that, they're usually referring to thinking in a creative and unconventional way. Specifically, the phrase refers to solving the "Nine Dots Puzzle," which requires that you not be constrained by the putative box formed by the nine dots. I failed that puzzle, so I guess I'm not creative. Golly, aren't tests grand? (I have some more thoughts on that topic below.)

Now I'm going to talk about an entirely different box, and I'm going to encourage you to think *inside* it as a way of exploring and developing collaborative creativity. The Box is a splendid old activity that probably is almost as old as boxes themselves and began as a children's game or just a way to pass a quiet evening.

There are generally two players in The Box. I call one the explorer and one the guide. The premise is that the explorer is standing in front of an imaginary box, exploring its contents. The guide asks questions about the box and what's inside it, and the explorer answers verbally and/or mimes the response.

What's the box made of? What color is it? What does it smell like? What sounds are coming from it? What's the first thing your hand touches when you reach inside the box? Is that object hot or cold? What does it taste like? Maybe the guide suggests an animal is in the box. What is it? What song is the animal singing?

The activity works best when the questions focus on immediate and sensory concepts rather than on narrative. Asking how the box arrived takes the players away from the goal of the activity, mutual immediate exploration, and has them instead focus on individual invention. "There's a card that says who sent the box; what does it say?" works better than, "Why would someone in Toledo send you this?"

There's only one wrong answer in The Box: "I don't know." Why? Because it's the explorer's box, and it doesn't really exist, so the explorer can make it anything. So can the guide, but the guide is really more of a servant to the explorer's vision.

The Box develops creativity for the participants as individuals and as a team. Ideally, the guide and explorer work together, feeding off one another. At times the guide is leading the explorer, but the guide is also following the explorer, building off the explorer's ideas. Neither party should dominate. In many ways it's like the mirroring exercise, only with words and specific concepts.

As usual in improv, you're looking to maximize the yeses and minimize the nos. If the explorer says there's a rubber ball in the box, the guide shouldn't say, "No, it's not a rubber ball." The ball's there; explore it. Maybe the guide can suggest that the ball is changing into another object or that there's something else in the box. The guide should try not to impose their ideas or control the explorer.

The explorer should likewise play nice. If the explorer discovers a dirty sock and the guide instructs the explorer to smell it, they should just go ahead and smell it. After all, it isn't real. The guide can even make this more palatable by suggesting, "It smells like something wonderful." I've had explorers tell me there's no way they're going to touch, smell, or taste some ostensibly offensive imaginary object. That'd be crazy! But who's the crazy one? Why not taste an imaginary mouse turd? Or maybe the explorers are so committed to what they're doing that it becomes real to them. That's cool too, I suppose.

Both players need to balance flexibility with assertiveness. They have to use their partner's suggestions. At the same time, they have to offer their own. There's no free lunch here. Everyone has to bring something to the table. The Box depends on cooperation and collaboration.

This game can be challenging, particularly for beginners. Usually the novice guide has the most difficulty because all the explorer has to do is answer questions. The struggling guide often can't think of any questions to ask, especially about the contents of the box. Or the guide just passes the buck by asking overly open questions like, "What is that thing?" which puts the creative onus on the explorer. Frustrated, the guide often has the explorer leave the box behind, and soon the explorer is wandering around inside a house or a forest, dealing with environments instead of objects. That's not a terrible thing, but it's not The Box.

The Box demands some discipline. You and your partner need to explore fully the premise you've created and not just abandon it once you're past the most immediate, easiest discoveries. You can always find something else in The Box. If you've gotten down to a tiny stone, it can be explored through all the senses, and, because it's not real, you can invoke magic; the stone can come to life or transform if it's thrown on the floor or into the air. The possibilities are limited only by your imaginations, which is to say that they're not limited at all. But you have to stay focused and keep digging. Discovery is *through* The Box, not outside of it.

You might have already seen how Yes-And is important in The Box. But there is a different aspect to Yes-And here, and the best way I can describe it is by introducing the concepts of "color" and "advance." In Yes-And Story, players are usually focused on advancing the action or plot. They spend little time coloring the details. The Box, however, is all about coloring because it's static and there is no plot. (I've included an activity called "Color/Advance" below.)

Play The Box for three to five minutes, stop, and discuss how it's going. If players report they were surprised by what happened, that's good. Surprises mean that neither player is controlling the other and that they're getting outside of the known and familiar by building off each other. Have the players trade roles and play for three to five minutes again. Ask the players how their first effort was different from their second.

As I said, The Box probably started out as a children's game, and, when I watch adults play it, I'm amazed at how childlike they look. It's a room of people *playing*, and I imagine they looked much the same when they were five years old, just less hairy. As children we created without self-consciousness, which develops later. As children we didn't define ourselves as creative or noncreative; we just *played*.

The best theatrical improvisers can make a scene out of just about anything because they pay attention to everything and can see the potential, mundane or sublime, in it. A fellow player's gesture or the mention of a seemingly minor detail can be the foundation of a scene. The players must simply observe something, endow it with meaning, and commit to that significance.

Improvisers struggle when they abandon what they've established, looking outside of it to make the scene work. An example of this that I've seen many, many times is when players decide to leave the location of a scene. "Let's go to the store," a player might suggest (and it always seems to be the store; I'm not sure why). The *character* might want to go to the store, but that merely reflects the *player's* desire to get the hell out of the scene, to be anywhere other than where they are. This desire can become desperate because no one wants to be stuck in a situation with no idea of what to do next. The unknown can be frightening. Rather than calmly observing what's happening and ascribing significance to it, players get all left-brained and start trying to invent their way out of their pickle. Pickles aren't scary to good improvisers; they're tempting.

Digging and exploring, striving to be aware of and to exploit potential exists outside of improvisational theater. Herman Melville tells you everything you could possibly want (and plenty you don't want) to know about whales in *Moby Dick*. The great saxophonist Sonny Rollins also springs to mind. Here's a guy who could find so many ways to render a simple tune that it could take him up to 20 minutes to get all the juice out of a melody. Honestly, that's a little extreme for me, but I'm trying to make a point here.

Beyond the arts, scientists, for instance, can't just walk away from research because they don't know where it's going. Their job isn't to *know* anyway; it's to observe and to learn. Figuring out what questions to ask is as important as finding the answers. I think this is what Einstein, a scientist you might have heard of, meant when he stated, "Imagination is more important than knowledge."

Ideation, innovation, and problem-solving often require that you address the issue at hand repeatedly. The key might not be immediately evident, or you might need to try a different approach or get another's perspective. In solving a crossword or assembling a jigsaw puzzle, you might move to another section if you're stymied, but moving to an entirely different puzzle doesn't get you anywhere with the first puzzle. Bang your head against the wall for a while, and, if that doesn't work, try your knee or a chair. Or a box. Or bang on the floor or the ceiling. (My legal representative advises me to clarify that I'm speaking in metaphor here.)

I think most of us put a boundary around our creative potential. Our self-made box makes us give up too quickly when our imaginations are challenged and we've picked the low-hanging fruit. Sometimes we allow an external boundary to be put around our creativity through testing, such as the Nine Dots Puzzle I mentioned. I've worked with so many people who solemnly intone their Myers-Briggs acronyms as if that chiseled in marble who they are and shall be. "Well, I'm an adapter, not an innovator," someone might say.

And I say who gives a fuck.

Look, I get that we crave external affirmation and even definition. There are major questions about the legitimacy of Myers-Briggs,[16] but it's still kind of cool to answer some questions and see what they add up to, especially if they confirm what you already thought. Astrology and various other psychic readings have even less scientific legitimacy, but many of us eat that up. And that's okay, but my point is that you shouldn't let those external measurements define you. *You* should define you!

Yes, some people have more innate creativity than others. Some people can jump higher than others just because they were born that way. Some people are sopranos, and some are basses, and many of us who want to hit those notes are just never going to hit them no matter how hard we work. That doesn't mean we can't sing well, and a good choir requires diverse voices. A two-handed, 360-degree, behind-the-head dunk might not be in our repertoire, but it doesn't mean we can't be good basketball players and valued team members. You can work on developing creativity, and who knows how that will evolve. Maybe it turns out you can be an innovator *and* an adaptor.

Try doing The Box, whether it's at a theater rehearsal or in a staff meeting. You might be surprised at what comes from it. Just remember; when you're tempted to abandon it, instead go deeper into the box.

Exercises

Individual

Sorry, there's really no way to play The Box in solitaire version because you need another player to provide the element of surprise and lack of control. That said, you don't need a class or big group to play, just another player, perhaps a child, a friend, or a childhood friend.

You can also do a deep exploration by sitting down in front of an object and writing everything you can about it. Start simply with a coffee mug, vase, or, um, box. Write down every material quality you can about the object. When you feel you've exhausted that category, become fanciful and inventive. You can make up characters or a story connected to the object. Once you've explored a simple object, you can challenge yourself by doing the exercise with an entire room or a landscape.

Group

1. **The Box**

   This game is great in person or online. If you're in a virtual environment, encourage players to be physical and mime the objects they're exploring.

   A. Ask for a volunteer, and demonstrate The Box with the volunteer playing the role of explorer and you as guide. Make sure you are familiar and comfortable with the exercise before demonstrating it to a group.

   B. Ask the explorer questions about the imaginary box in front of them. Focus on the senses. The explorer can respond with words and/or actions.

   C. Play for three to five minutes, long enough to get a feel for the game but not so long that it becomes tiresome. Ask leading questions of the explorer, but don't try to control them or make them bring *your* vision to life. If you feel the explorer is getting complacent or merely describing something from their everyday life, try to shake things up. Neither player should feel that this activity is predictable.

   D. When you're done with the demonstration, ask the explorer how they did. Then ask the audience how they thought the explorer did. What specifically did the audience like? Ask the audience who was leading and who was following (the correct answer is "yes"). Ask the explorer where their ideas came from. Perhaps you can comment on your experience as guide.

   E. Break your group into pairs. If you have an odd number,

      make one team a trio and start them with two guides and one explorer. Ask if there are questions, answer any that arise, and have your teams play The Box. If you're in a virtual environment, send your subgroups into breakout rooms.

  F. After three to five minutes, stop the activity. Ask your group how the exercise is going. What are the challenges? Are there surprises?

  G. Have the players switch roles and repeat steps E and F. Before you move on to a new activity, be sure to ask your group about real-world applications of The Box.

2. **Create a Space One Object at a Time**

  A. This exercise works best with groups of eight or fewer. I doubt I'd try it online because spatial relationships are so important in this activity.

  B. Suggest or get a suggestion for a generic location. It could be a rec room, an office, a bar, or just about any place.

  C. The first player enters the imaginary location and creates an object. In a rec room it might be a foosball table; in a bar it might be a beer tap.

  D. Each subsequent player enters, handles the previous objects created (if they're not sure what the object is, they should mimic what they saw, and they'll either figure it out or look like they did), and creates a new object. To make things fairer and more challenging, you can have the players go twice in "snaking" order, so the first player winds up going last in the second iteration.

  E. Play again and/or process the activity. What were the challenges? What are the nontheatrical applications? If you plan to do scenes with your group, this exercise is a great way to emphasize space work (interacting with imaginary objects and settings) and paying attention to other players rather than merely focusing on one's own idea.

3. **Color/Advance** (good for in-person or virtual groups)

  A. You need one director and at least one storyteller, although you can have two to three.

  B. The storyteller(s) begin telling a story. It could be a fairy tale or recounting what they did last weekend.

    C. When the director wants more detail about something, perhaps a character, an object, or a place, they say, "Color." The storyteller then adds description.

    D. When the director is satisfied with the detail, they say, "Advance." Now the storyteller continues with the action or plot.

    E. Repeat until sated.

4. **Space Painting** (good for in-person or virtual groups)

    A. Ask for four volunteers, and give them a generic location such as a kitchen, a garage, or an office.

    B. Players take turns adding some element to the imaginary space. It might be a piece of furniture or a window. It could also be a sound, smell, or quality of light. Have them focus on inanimate objects; animals are okay, I suppose, but people are off limits because there will be a temptation to focus on story rather than space and also because the underlying idea here is to create a stage onto which actors enter. If you're in person, have the volunteers move to the exact place where the objects are that they're describing.

    C. Players should build off each other. If Player A describes a bookshelf, Player B can describe the books in it. If Player C describes a radio, Player D can describe what it's playing.

    D. Encourage players to add personal objects or maybe something that doesn't seem to belong to the space. This makes the space less sterile and adds dramatic potential and fun.

    E. Have each player contribute several elements to the setting. Having the players go in order is a good way to keep them from dominating or avoiding participation. That said, if the group is stuck or working very well together, allowing players to be motivated by inspiration is okay too.

    F. Repeat Space Painting a few times. It's great practice for awareness, additive creativity, and collaboration. As you process the exercise, a good question to ask is, "What do we know about the people who inhabit this space?" It's almost like detective work, and it reveals the way we synthesize information and incorporate intuition into that process.

5. **Space Painting into Scenes**

    A. A good introduction to scene work is a two-person version of Space Painting. Now two players will not only create the setting, just as above, but also perform a scene in it after they've created it.

    B. Again, part of this activity involves detective work. Once the scene has begun, the players should use the objects and allow the spatial elements to define their characters. It's an organic approach toward improvising that encourages collaborative discovery and limits egoistic invention.

11

The Myths of Perfection and Originality

"The artist who aims at perfection in everything achieves it in nothing."—Eugene Delacroix

Perfectionism and trying to be original are two impossible and worthless endeavors. Both can stifle our creativity and performances—even our very beings. The more one indulges perfectionism and pursuit of originality, the further one gets from the perfect and the original.

Now I'm not saying we shouldn't strive for excellence and be our true selves. Quite the opposite, I *am* saying we should do those things. But I'm also saying that the concepts of perfection and originality are not useful in and are probably detrimental to these efforts.

Almost all of my individual coaching and much of my group teaching eventually focuses on problems that arise from perfectionism and trying to be original. This chapter doesn't end with specific activities because you can apply the mindset I'm suggesting to any activity, or any activity can make you aware of your thinking on the subject.

You might be new to improv, in which case it's good to remind yourself to be in a learning, rather than a mastering frame of mind. The same applies if you're a teacher using this book as you lead new activities or old activities in new ways. Seeing as we're about halfway through this course, now seems like a good time for a pep talk.

For a theoretically good thing, perfection sure does cause a lot of trouble. Or maybe perfection's theoretical nature is itself the problem. Perfection doesn't exist except as a concept. To be entirely without defect or fault is impossible, at least for people, in part because judging perfection is subjective. I mean, a "perfect game" for a pitcher doesn't mean that they threw the ball 81 times and each batter whiffed on each pitch, right? In the 1976 Olympics, Nadia Comăneci earned not one but six "perfect 10" scores in gymnastics. Considering the advances in that sport, today's athletes should be earning 13s by those old standards.

Some see the impossibility of reaching perfection and don't even bother heading in its general direction, preferring to stay locked in stasis. Maybe they want to escape a bad job or relationship, or maybe they want to write a novel or play piano. There are so many paths they could take, but they don't take the first step down any path because none is flawless.

Sometimes people get discouraged because, once they start in a direction, the going or their performance isn't perfect, and good isn't good enough for them. Progress is incremental, and failure often precedes greater success. Doing poorly can be demoralizing and frustrating, but that's the price for improvement and progress.

Perfectionism and even just the desire to excel can seriously hinder students in various environments. It's good to want to do well, but when you're a student, just *doing* is enough. For example, I once had a student who had great difficulty embracing simple instructions like, "say yes" and "avoid conflict," which is fairly common. The student resisted, apparently convinced that it was impossible to do a good improv scene in a Pollyannaish world of agreement. He wanted to do an *excellent* scene, not an exercise for novices.

Yet once he finally trusted the process, focused on agreement, and avoided conflict, he did a wonderful scene and seemed somewhat stunned, almost as if he'd jumped off a cliff and found he could fly rather than merely plummeting. His scene partner seemed amazed too, and their scene, which was essentially a niceness contest, was terrific. Then the student decided this couldn't possibly last and introduced conflict, which promptly caused the scene to crash and burn. Introducing the conflict was a symptom of wanting to do better. "Striving to be better, we oft mar what's well," Shakespeare wrote.

At other times I've seen students succeed in an exercise or game and then start to struggle. When I've asked them about this, I've learned that they began to doubt themselves. They suspected they weren't doing well enough according to some mysterious standard. Although the standard is internal, the students have generally constructed it of external components, things they believe others believe. Moreover, the students admit they believe others hold them to this internal standard.

If this sounds complicated, it is! This is what improvisers mean by "being in your head," and you can see where this kind of neurotic, if understandable, behavior can hurt your performance, whether or not it's improv.

When students bail out of whatever they're doing well, afraid they're failing, the audience is almost always disappointed—not with what the students were doing but that they stopped doing it! The lack of perfection was good enough for the audience (and me) but not for the performer.

So perfection is not only impossible to achieve, but it's also difficult to define, and then you have to figure out whose definition it is. Who sets the standard, and what are their qualifications? If someone calls something perfect, would the creator, who knows all its flaws and the failure that went into it, agree?

If there is perfection in this world, I believe it's akin to the Japanese concept of *wabi-sabi*, which essentially means beauty in imperfection. This perfection is flawed but perfect *because* of its flaws, not in spite of them. This perfection is organic and comes from within rather than without. It's the perfection we can see in nature.

We can see it elsewhere too. For example, when trumpeter Miles Davis played, his notes sometimes slid and cracked, and yet these flaws gave his playing a poignant sensitivity. Igor Stravinsky and Thelonious Monk wrote amazing music that often feels like it has "wrong" notes or rhythms. Louis Armstrong, Janis Joplin, and Bob Dylan are great singers who are far from operatically perfect. These artists' personalities and heart are augmented by their imperfections.

Then there's the painter, Fra Lippo Lippi, immortalized in the eponymous poem by Robert Browning.[17] His paintings were considered "too perfect" and to lack human feeling and thus were not celebrated as much as those by less perfectionistic artists. It's from this poem that we get perhaps the most useful concept of perfection, "Ah, but a man's reach should exceed his grasp, or what's a heaven for?"

Contrast Lippi's works to those of Vincent van Gogh, which were initially criticized as technically incorrect and rejected by critics and patrons. The paint, after all, is piled on the canvas, the images are often crude, and the perspective is occasionally awry. Yet stand in front of one of van Gogh's great works and see if its passion doesn't transport you. There's emotional truth and power there that transcend realism. The perfection is the imperfection or vice versa. Critics, patrons, and the general public came to appreciate that, alas a bit too late for Vincent.

It's worth noting that some cultures consider it an affront to the divine to strive for perfection, and so, even in their finest work, artists and craftspeople deliberately build in a flaw as an act of humility and reverence. Both Persian and Navajo rugmakers, for example, include a deliberate flaw in their work—although the inevitable accidental flaws likely make the ritual redundant.

I'd even go so far as to say that flaws make people lovable, just as vulnerability makes them trustworthy (a concept I'll explore in a later chapter). I call these imperfections the "barbs of love" because you get stuck on them, almost against your will. I've had friends and pets who had some foible that, though annoying, ultimately made me feel more connected to them. And we all know people who, while perhaps not quite "ugly sexy," appeal to us more powerfully than traditional beauties. Perfection, if it existed, would be boring!

Maybe Lorenz Hart's lyrics (to Richard Rodgers' music) say it best:
"Your looks are laughable
Unphotographable
Yet you're my favorite work of art."

Mistakes and shortcomings can lend authenticity and dynamism to improv and other performances. Certainly those delivering planned or scripted performances want to avoid having them seem "canned." I've even been told that my company should make *more* mistakes and thus make improvising look harder so that audiences can believe we're making it all up and have greater appreciation for what we're doing! It's ironic that outstanding improv is so seamless it appears scripted, while outstanding scripted work is so fresh it appears improvised.

Good improvisers know that they will never do a "perfect" show. Someone will get a character's name wrong or commit some technical glitch. There are always missed opportunities. But if they focus on good technique, collaborate playfully, and concentrate on what they're doing rather than on an ambiguous external standard, they can create wonderful performances that are perfect in their own right.

"The thing that is really hard, and really amazing, is giving up on being perfect and beginning the work of becoming yourself," wrote author Anna Quindlen.

GREATNESS
Always be a first-rate version of yourself and not a second rate version of someone else.—Judy Garland

A discussion of perfectionism doesn't seem quite perfect without exploring perceptions of greatness. We tend to exalt established, recognized performers and artists. Who are we to dare to be funny or sing, write, or paint—to create—when others are clearly more accomplished than we are? Well, just because someone does something better than we do it doesn't mean we shouldn't do it at all. We shouldn't avoid playing tennis just because there are players who are good enough to make a living at it. Maybe you'll never be great at something, but that doesn't mean you shouldn't do it. And, of course, you'll never have a chance to become great at something at all *unless* you do it.

What is artistic or performative greatness anyway? What is success in these areas? Just as with the examples from baseball and gymnastics I mentioned, it's difficult and maybe even impossible to measure these things quantitatively. Assuming a basic level of competence, much reaction to performance and art comes down to subjective taste. While tastes can be cultivated, people like what they like.

More than once I've seen music and dance concerts by internationally recognized, critically acclaimed artists. I knew they were good, and I tried to like them but just couldn't find my way there. When the rest of the audience was standing for an ovation, I was standing so I could find the nearest exit. I've also been at improv shows that I would describe as "bad" or at least "cheap" and seen most of the audience roaring with laughter and apparently having a great time. Were they wrong? Was I? I can only say that our reactions were different.

Often success and greatness have as much to do with luck, connections, and persistence as they do with talent. For example, there are good actors *everywhere*. The ones you see on screen might be very talented or maybe only moderately so. Maybe they have little more than "the look" a casting agent is seeking. That actor might have merely been in the right place at the right time, known someone, or devoted their life to getting such roles rather than following another path. That actor might have no better dramatic skills than someone you might see in a small, local production.

Greatness is everywhere—as is mediocrity. You might pay top dollar to see a musical act on tour, but it doesn't mean that musician is better than the one playing in the coffeehouse or subway stop. (Sometimes you might even see the same musician on tour *and* busking on the street.) What's important is *doing* something. Do it if you're not great, do it if you are great, do it and maybe you'll become great (whether or not anyone recognizes it).

ORIGINALITY

Why should we not also enjoy an original relationship with the universe?—Ralph Waldo Emerson

Just as is the case with being perfect, many of us want to be original. Originality is both impossible and unavoidable, so striving for it is pointless. The very notion that we can create or do something completely original is preposterous when you think of it. The most brilliant inventors are building off the ideas of others. Artists and designers on the sharpest cutting edges are also inspired by, incorporate, and even react in opposition to artists and designers who preceded them.

Fittingly I'm not the first to suggest this. Mark Twain addressed this concept in a letter to Helen Keller in 1903:

> For substantially all ideas are second-hand, consciously and unconsciously drawn from a million outside sources, and daily used by the garnerer with a pride and satisfaction born of the superstition that he originated them; whereas there is not a rag of originality about them anywhere except the little discoloration they get from his mental and moral calibre and his temperament, and which is revealed in characteristics of phrasing. When a great orator makes a great speech you are listening to ten centuries and ten thousand men—but we call it *his* speech, and really some exceedingly small portion of it *is* his.... It takes a thousand men to invent a telegraph, or a steam engine, or a phonograph, or a telephone or any other important thing—and the last man gets the credit and we forget the others.[18]

And yet....

For all the billions of people who inhabit the earth and the billions more who have come and gone before us, there is no one *exactly* like us. Our DNA, experiences, education, relationships, and cultures combine to make us unique, despite our many similarities. Therefore, we can't help but be original if we are true to ourselves.

And yet....

Much of the way we learn is through imitation. As infants we mimic the movement and sounds others around us make and thus figure out how to walk and talk. Later we're influenced by others in the way we write, dance, throw a ball, or smoke a cigarette. We reflect our teachers, be they coaches or just people we've seen in person or on screen.

And yet....

Over time we start rebelling against our earlier models, most often our parents. Adolescence is defined in part by this. We're trying to be original, not defined by others. Of course, striving *not* to be like someone else is being influenced by that person just as much as striving *to* be like that person is.

And yet....

No two people share the exact complex set of influences. And no matter how hard we try, we can't exactly replicate our influences. Pianist Herbie Hancock, considered an originator in musical styles as diverse as jazz, hip-hop, and pop, described his surprise when he read a review early in his career that mentioned his style. Hancock, who was still working a day gig as a mail carrier, thought he was just borrowing stylistic and technical elements from other musicians. But obviously the critic who wrote the review heard something new in the mélange Hancock assembled.

This story is not unique. Just about any artist or athlete can identify models they tried to copy. I've seen musical "family trees" that trace the branches of influences. For instance, Billie Holiday influenced Frank Sinatra, who influenced Johnny Hartman, and yet they all sound very different most of the time.

As a singer I constantly cop turns of phrase from other singers. I'm especially fond of borrowing from female singers like Dinah Washington, Sarah Vaughan, and Rosemary Clooney, in no small part because what I'm borrowing will sound so different and even original in my voice. With most songs, after much repetition, I forget who influenced me; the song takes on its own life, and I wind up singing it the way I sing it. Sometimes I listen to a recording that I originally mimicked, and I'm astonished to hear how different it is from how my version has evolved.

I experienced a similar process when I began teaching decades ago. At first I felt I was just copying teachers I thought were good. This bothered me at first because it felt almost like plagiarism, and my ego also wanted to leave its specific mark. But my goal was to teach well, so I focused on that, and my self-consciousness about imitating others dissipated, no doubt due in part to my finding and developing my own teaching style.

Sometimes in class a student will borrow a character, joke, or idea from a popular TV show or movie, appropriating something they're confident will get a positive response. That's certainly understandable. (Indeed, when I was 15, I spent about a third of my time imitating Steve Martin, a third imitating Bill Murray, and a third imitating myself.)

Thus, we encounter the border between being influenced by and imitating someone. The former is probably essential and never quite disappears, while the latter might be a necessary starting point but should be quickly discarded.

The problem with sustained imitation is that we don't hear the voice of the individual but rather a second-rate version of someone else. Sustained imitation reflects a lack of confidence in one's ideas and talents. These ideas don't feel original or creative to the individual because they live with them all the time and can't recognize their originality and creativity. Familiarity breeds contempt, right? Based on my experience and observations, I suspect this applies even more to oneself than to others.

"You're all weird," I find myself saying to students. "And that's a good thing because that's where your unique creativity and value come from. Your job is to become aware of that weirdness and use it! And it doesn't matter if that happens on stage or in a board room."

It's impossible to please everyone, so you might as well try to appeal to those who are inclined to like you and what you're doing. This is a long way of saying, "Be yourself." Be your original, derivative, perfect, flawed self. Being rejected for who you really are hurts more than superficial rejection, but I'd say the potential reward of being liked for who you are is worth the risk and vastly better than being liked for who you aren't.

If you're a teacher or director, be vigilant for the symptoms of perfectionism and striving for originality. Ask questions when you think you see these issues, which often manifest as impostor syndrome (which we'll explore in the next chapter). You might be surprised at how many people are striving to be perfect and/or original. Let them talk.

Exercises

Individual

Think about and maybe write down the ways in which you pursue perfection and originality. Do they help you? Do they make you happy? How do they affect other people? Remember, we're not talking about striving for excellence here but rather the pursuit of perfection and originality. Even so, your list might not be comprised of exclusively bad things.

Group

Talk about and maybe write down the ways in which you pursue perfection and originality. Do they help you? Do they make you happy? How do they affect other people? Remember, we're not talking about striving for excellence here but rather the pursuit of perfection and originality. Even so, your list might not be comprised of exclusively bad things.

12

All Systems Go

"Know thyself."—Socrates

Some people say that 93 percent of the meaning you convey is based on how you say it, that verbal content comprises only 7 percent of your message. How amazing!

Alas, those people are wrong. The number is a common misinterpretation of research by Albert Mehrabian examined in his 1971 book, *Silent Messages.*[19] That said, I think we can all agree that *how* you say something is very important and may even be more important than *what* you say. Put another way, your delivery of your message has a huge effect on how your message is received. Furthermore, the way you appear and sound plays an essential part in how your character is perceived, whether it's a fictional persona onstage or who you actually are in your professional or social life.

For these reasons we focus intensely on physicality in acting, both scripted and improvised, and in my applied improv classes and workshops. Physicality, for the purposes of this discussion, covers posture, gesture, facial expression, and breathing. Physicality is even important when your audience can't see you because it affects the way you speak and sound. Speech and voice are physical processes, so we'll also touch on them.

In a previous chapter I introduced physicality as a crucial aspect of improv and performance. In this chapter we'll focus sharply on physical awareness and presence. This focus is a holistic approach, connecting body, thoughts, and emotions, and is at the heart of my performing and presentation technique.

Breath

If I plan to focus on breathing in a session, I like to begin with an active game of some sort. Then I have everyone find a spot where they can lie down on their backs. If someone doesn't want to lie down on the floor, they can lie down on a table, counter, or some other furniture. I take great pride in turning a graduate-level class-room into something that resembles kindergarten with students running around and then lying down for what a surprise visitor might take to be nap time.

Once everyone is recumbent, we put one hand over our navels and notice the way our bellies rise and fall as we inhale and exhale. To heighten awareness of their breathing, I instruct participants to breathe in through their noses and out through their mouths. Eventually I have participants see how high they can make the hand on their bellies rise by taking in the biggest breaths they can.

Next I have participants place their free hand at the very top of their chests. Now they breathe in with a wave of air filling their torsos, starting at the belly and moving up to the chest. The wave recedes and the chest falls, followed by the belly. I want them to be deliberate in their breathing and will give some coaching if I see there are problems. Part of my goal is to get people to engage their diaphragms, which this exercise does, but any awareness of breathing is good. After a few minutes I have everyone rise *slowly* (so as to avoid blacking out) to their feet and gather in a circle.

I explain that we're focusing on breathing because it's good for the presenter and good for the audience. Breath control is essential to vocal stamina, projection, and resonance. It also keeps you from having to take a breath in the middle of a (breath) sentence or even in the mid–(breath)-dle of a word. I note that people whose voices get tired easily probably don't have a problem with their vocal cords so much as they don't support their voices with proper breathing.

While standing we try to recreate the "wave of air" that we did lying on our backs. It's harder to do while on your feet, but some people get it right away. Sticking out your tongue and panting is another way of engaging the diaphragm—and simultaneously losing all dignity. As with so many things, practice is key; I didn't master engaging my diaphragm until I was in my 20s and after many acting and singing lessons.

There is a deeper aspect to breathing too. When we're under

stress, we often experience instinctual fight or flight responses. These responses manifest in many ways, including faster and shallower breathing, heightened blood pressure and heart rate, and in extreme cases tunnel vision and loss of motor control. These responses obviously served our species well when the need to fight or flee was more frequent, but they're overkill and even counterproductive in situations like being asked a question you didn't expect in a meeting, reciting a monologue, or going to chat with that cute so-and-so at the bar.

When our bodies are going berserk, our brains will follow. It's called panic. So it behooves us to master ways of calming our bodies in hopes that our minds remain calm as well. For me (and many, many others), this calmness starts with slowing and deepening one's breath. Your pulse rate and blood pressure will drop if you can modulate your breathing.[20] You'll get more oxygen into your system, which your brain and body need. It's the most effective non-medicinal anxiety intervention I know of, and, let's face it, popping a handful of pills or shooting oneself with a tranquilizer dart can raise eyebrows and create an unwanted chemical dependence.

There are so many things in the world that we can't control, but breathing is usually one thing we can, and thus it's the first step in what I call the Systems Check, which some people refer to as the Body Scan Meditation.

Body

Once we know we're breathing—and I've known people who actually hold their breath under pressure, which is not a practice I recommend—we can take a larger look at our entire body. I like to start at the base:

- Are your feet firmly on the ground and is your weight balanced on them? The sides of one's ankles are not meant to be stood upon, but I've seen plenty of speakers roll their feet over so that they're doing just that. I've also seen speakers actually lose their balance and start to fall because they're not grounded. Everything your body is doing starts with your footwork. You can be picking up a box or going for a high note in a song; either way, you've got to support that effort by being balanced and grounded, giving the rest of your body a solid foundation for whatever it's about to do.

• Are your knees locked? Just to be sure, lock your knees until you feel your quadriceps tighten. Now relax your quads and release your knees, so you know the difference between locked and loose. Most people who have been in the military, a marching band, a wedding party, or a military marching-band wedding party will tell you that you can pass out if you lock your knees.[21] While you might not reach the point of passing out from locking your knees, having suppleness in your legs helps with balance and posture and keeps muscle groups relaxed instead of tense.

• Are your quads tight? What about your glutes? Are you sucking your bootie into your body? Relax those legs! Free that ass! Subsuming one's buttocks into the torso has an adverse effect on breathing and speaking and doesn't look or feel good.

• Is your back straight, like Momma told you to keep it? Dancers are often taught to imagine a string pulling the top of their head toward the ceiling. This not only helps you stand straight and to your full height; it helps to align the spine in a way that helps the shoulders to drop down and back, allowing the chest to open for better breathing and keeps the chin from jutting out and up.

• Are your shoulders up by your ears, or are they low and relaxed? Think about those roadside signs that read "Soft shoulder" and heed their advice. Let your arms hang loose and heavy; bring the shoulders down. You might shake them out a bit.

• What's going on with your face? Is your jaw clenched? Are you squinting? Is your brow furrowed?

It takes a lot longer to read the Systems Check[22] than it does to run through it, especially if you make a habit of doing it. I'm a seasoned veteran of performing and teaching, and I still get anxious when I'm in front of an audience. So I use this technique, and it works for me, both in preparation and in the midst of performance when I use it to get grounded or back to home base. It doesn't always solve my problems, but it helps me to be in the best possible condition, both how I feel and how I appear, and to handle any issues that might arise. I can't promise the Systems Check will work for you, but it's the best thing I can recommend.

Voice

Once we're where we want to be with our breath and bodies, we can focus on voice and elements of speech. A voice supported by breath and body can function effectively for hours, and that means stamina, projection, and volume. Just make sure you're not putting all the burden on your vocal cords and to warm up your voice before you perform or present.

Here are some other important things to consider, both in preparation and while presenting.

- **Pace**. So many people talk too fast and are thus less intelligible and expressive than those who speak at a moderate pace. What's the point of speaking if your audience can't understand you? And if you rush your speech, you're also sending the message, whether or not it's true, that you're anxious. If you seem anxious, you'll seem less confident, and talking too fast can even make it seem like you're rushing to get your insignificant message out of the way. Speaking fast often leads to loss of breath control so that the speaker needs a breath at the wrong time or has to swallow a word, which always looks painful to me. So slow down. Slooooow down. Inveterate speed-talkers need constant reminders to slow down, in part because a slower pace will feel very odd and make them feel insecure. I can't remember ever coaching a speaker who needed to speed up, while at least half of the speakers I coach could go slower. That said, don't drag things out and take unearned pauses— unless you're a really fast talker and you need to practice speaking slower.
- **Enunciation**. Americans are great at vowels but often not so adept with consonants. Well, we're not the only ones, I suppose. As a bartender in London, I once took an order for "free poi's uh bi-uh." I informed the patron that pints of bitter were a pound each, at which point he gave me the look of sourest disdain, held up three fingers, and said, *"Free,*

not free." But I digress. Apart from slowing down, nothing will make your speech more easily understood than hitting those consonants. Slightly exaggerating your t's, d's, and such might make you feel like you're overdoing it, but I suspect you're likely to hear less "huh, what?" from your audiences. And you might just sound more erudite. Some people feel they're putting on airs when they enunciate clearly. But just because you're intelligible and intelligent doesn't mean you're pretentious or bombastic. Living in an ironic age makes most of us so worried that we're somehow being uncool that we slide into sloppiness.

- **Pitch**. The word monotony means both "boredom" and "of one pitch." The human voice is capable of an astonishing range of notes. Spend time around a baby, and prepare to be amazed. Speaking requires us to modulate our pitch. Unfortunately, many of us modulate the life right out of our speech. That not only makes us boring, but also, again, makes us harder to understand. Emphasizing a word or phrase with pitch or notes that are different from the rest of the sentence conveys meaning. The speaker suggests to the listener not only that something is significant but how they should feel about that information. I'm not saying we should sing when we're speaking (and I understand that not all languages use pitch in the ways that English does), but if you're not using a variety of pitches, you're leaving expressive potential on the table. Yet beware of using the same pitch over and over. Some of us, for instance, repeatedly inflect the end of our sentences upwards so that it seems like we're asking question after question. This doesn't make us sound confident.

- **Timbre**. Just as an orchestra has many instruments that make different qualities of sound, so do people have voices that sound different. Some of us are French horns while others are flutes. And some of us are circular saws or leaf blowers. Some voices sound so pleasant that I'm more inclined to listen to what they're saying. They often convey confidence or calm. I'm not trying to be prescriptive here, but I want you to know that you can experiment with vocal tone. If you like the way someone's voice sounds, try imitating it (just not in front of them). I used to do a lot of

studio voice work, usually as a "character," meaning that
the way my voice sounded had to suggest a persona. So I
might adopt a nasal twang, a high-pitched, naïve tone, or
maybe a smooth and sophisticated voice. There's no "right"
way to sound, but you can experiment with it. Just beware
that if you're working on tone by recording yourself, almost
no one likes the sound of their recorded voice, so don't be
discouraged.

• **Vocal clutter**. Like, um, try not to, like, do it, ya know? That
said, if you've got something important to say and you're
saying it well, a little clutter isn't going to ruin your message
except for the dedicated pedants in the audience. So don't be
too hard on yourself. Ya know?

We are a world of people making unconscious movements. We
twiddle, twirl, and scratch. We tap, drum, and stroke. There's nothing necessarily wrong with all that except that it can detract from a
message you're trying to convey or even send a message that's opposite the one you intend.

There are many ways of saying the same words. The same scene
in a play can have widely different effects based on the way the lines
are delivered. (We'll explore this phenomenon later.) The same is
true of speeches. Imagine Martin Luther King, Jr.'s, "I Have a Dream"
speech[23] delivered by someone slouching over a podium, one foot
raised behind them, and looking down at a script.

All this is true of improvisation too—except that there is one
enormous difference. There is no script to rely on in improv, so what
you say is largely dependent on how you're behaving physically. Your
body and voice affect the content of your speech and the character
you're trying to portray, and this is true if you're doing an improv
scene in a theater or answering a tough, unexpected question in a
boardroom. (We'll also explore this phenomenon later.)

So what are you doing right now? What are your fingers and toes
doing? Your mouth and your eyebrows? What's your posture? I don't
want you to feel bad, and it's not Red Light, Green Light, so I won't
send you back to the start of this section if you're moving. I just want
you to be aware and in control. Master those things now, and later
we'll delve deeply into being *deliberate*, making conscious choices
about how to use physicality to make your communication more
effective.

Exercises

Individual

1. **Focused Breathing**
    A. Find a comfortable place to lie down on your back with your legs straight.
    B. Put your hand over your navel, and, breathing in through your nose and out through your mouth, notice the way your belly rises and falls with inhaling and exhaling.
    C. See how high you can make the hand on your belly rise by taking in the biggest breath you can and also how low your hand can go as you completely exhale.
    D. Place your free hand at the very top of your chest, and breathe in with a wave of air filling your torso, starting at the belly and moving up through the chest. The wave recedes and the chest falls, followed by the belly. Repeat until you don't want to do it anymore.
    E. Slowly rise to your feet.
    F. Try to recreate the "wave of air" while standing.
    G. Stick out your tongue, and pant to engage your diaphragm.
2. Every time you notice or check the time also take notice of your body. Imagine yourself taking a selfie, and think how it would look.
3. Try to be aware of nervous habits you have. Do you tap your toes, twirl your hair? You don't have to stop doing these things; just be aware of them.
4. In your interactions with other people, take notice of your physicality. Try not to get too distracted, but ask yourself if there might be a more effective way of presenting yourself when you're speaking or listening. Does your body match the message you're trying to convey? Can you enhance the message physically?
5. **Systems Check**
    You can do the following exercise anywhere, and you can do it standing, sitting, or in just about any position. Waiting in line somewhere? Put your phone away, and do the Systems Check! Or do it without putting your phone away; it'll only take a few seconds.

    A. Stand with your weight evenly balanced on both feet, which should be about shoulder-width apart.

    B. Lock knees. Then release. Lock and release. Then bounce slightly.

    C. Move your focus up your legs and into the torso, being aware of balance and tension in the body. Relax tight muscles.

    D. Focus on posture. Stand up straight, and notice the way your shoulders and jaw drop and your chest opens as you stand tall.

    E. Let your arms hang heavy and loose, again keeping your shoulders low and relaxed.

    F. Relax your face, and be aware of clenching your jaw and other tension in the neck and head.

6. Sing. Sing in the car. Sing in the shower. Sing while you're doing yardwork. Nothing makes you more aware of what your voice can do than singing does. Identify the song's emotions, and try to bring them to life. Focus on singing the lyrics clearly; it's good practice for enunciating while speaking.

7. Work on your consonants. Say this sequence out loud: "Puh-puh-puh-puh-puh. Buh-buh-buh-buh-buh. Tuh-tuh-tuh-tuh-tuh. Duh-duh-duh-duh-duh. Kuh-kuh-kuh-kuh-kuh. Guh-guh-guh-guh-guh. Qua-qua-qua-qua-qua." Notice that the "puh" sound is explosive, and the subsequent sounds are less so until "qua" is almost implosive swallowing. Notice the position of the lips, teeth, and tongue as you make these sounds. This is a great warm-up for speakers and also reminds us to be aware of speaking clearly.

8. The world's simplest vocal warm-up is simply humming. You know how you nod your head and say "uh-hmmm" (gee, that's hard to spell) when you're agreeing with someone? Do that several times. It'll knock a little rust off the vocal cords and help to keep your voice from sounding raspy (especially if you've been sleeping) and also keep your voice from cracking. Of course, you can be more elaborate with your vocal warm-up, and you can find exercises easily. I'm a big fan of getting my vocal cords warm and flexible so that they're ready to do what I ask of them. And just as you can injure your body by straining it when it's not prepared, so can you injure your voice.

Group

All of the following exercises can be done online. The leader might not be able to see much of what is going on with participants but can still offer verbal coaching. Lag rules out unison speaking and singing, but you can still do call and response in virtual environments.

1. **Focused Breathing**
    A. Participants find a comfortable place to lie down on their backs with their legs straight.
    B. Participants put their hand over their navels, and, breathing in through the nose and out through the mouth, notice the way their bellies rise and fall with inhaling and exhaling.
    C. Participants see how high they can make the hand on their bellies rise by taking in the biggest breaths they can and also how low their hands can go as they completely exhale.
    D. Participants place their free hand at the very top of their chests and breathe in with a wave of air filling their torsos, starting at the belly and moving up through the chest. The wave recedes and the chest falls, followed by the belly.
    E. Participants slowly get to their feet.
    F. Discuss the experience and the importance of purposeful breathing.
    G. Participants try to recreate the "wave of air" while standing.
    H. Participants stick out their tongues and pant to engage their diaphragms.

2. **Systems Check**
    A. Participants stand with their weight evenly balanced on both feet, which should be about shoulder-width apart.
    B. Lock knees. Then release. Lock and release. Then bounce slightly.
    C. Move focus up the legs and into the torso, being aware of balance and tension in the body. Relax tight muscles.
    D. Focus on posture. Stand up straight, and notice the way the shoulders and jaw drop and the chest opens as we stand tall.

    E. Let the arms hang heavy and loose, again keeping our shoulders low and relaxed.

    F. Relax the face, and be aware of clenching the jaw and other tension in the neck and head.

3. **Vocal Warm-ups**

   Use those mentioned in the individual exercises section above or bring your own. You can even sing a song. People usually feel more comfortable singing as a group than solo.

4. Ask participants about what they do to prepare and focus. What warm-ups do they do? Perhaps someone has special expertise they can share. For example, I've had doctors, athletes, special-forces veterans, and Broadway performers lend their perspectives and advice, and I'm grateful for it. Warm-ups are useful not just in and of themselves but also as preparation rituals.

13

Act Authoritatively, Be Authoritative

"I have written 11 books, but each time I think, 'Uh oh, they're going to find out now. I've run a game on everybody, and they're going to find me out.'"
—Maya Angelou

Conveying authority is a problem for many of us. We have the expertise, but we often simply feel and behave as though we don't. This is known as impostor syndrome, and it can cause us a lot of misery and even failure.

Impostor syndrome is complex and can be caused by a variety of things. Some of us don't "own" our expertise because we're aware that others know more about our specialties than we do—which, ironically, is an indication of how much we *do* know. Some of us are so aware of how people and circumstances have helped us succeed that we discount our own contributions.

Regardless of its roots, the impostor syndrome is one we would do well to address and try to overcome.[24] Counterintuitively, playing the role of actual impostor can help in this effort. Expert Interview is an old standard for improv actors, and it's also extremely useful for people in nontheatrical settings. This game builds on the Systems Check from the previous chapter. Whereas we were looking to increase physical awareness and readiness, to create a blank slate if you will, now we're looking to be deliberate in the way we're using our bodies.

To start Expert Interview I have three volunteers sit in chairs in front of the rest of the group. (I'll add a fourth volunteer if they seem especially eager or if there's a chance to increase diversity on the panel.) "We're gonna have a TV talk show!" I say. "I'm the host, and these are my guests. Why are they on my show? Because they're experts! And what are they experts in? Whatever we, the audience, tell them. So even if you actually know nothing about being an astronaut or a choreographer or whatever, you can answer any question we put to you. There's only one wrong answer and that's 'I don't know.'"

Before we get our audience suggestions, I give my players three directions:

1. The moment we tell you what your expertise is, think how that person would sit. What's your posture? What are you doing with your feet and your hands? What's the expression on your face? Maybe you can even think about what this person might be wearing. Don't worry about being original or trite; just go with the first thing that comes to mind.

2. Remember to breathe. Indeed, if you find yourself wondering what questions we'll ask you, which you absolutely cannot control, focus on your breathing, which is something you can control. You might even find some character trait in your breathing, something I've seen often in shows and classes.

3. Commit to what you're doing. Rather than worrying if it's right or wrong or whether or not the audience likes it, just stick with your character. Remember this is just a game, and you're not supposed to be an actual expert. We're pretending, and it'll be more fun for you and everyone else if you don't bail out of your character. When in doubt, give it the gas, not the brake.

Then we get our suggestions, and off we go. I'll ask questions first and later open it up to the audience's questions. I go first because I want the players to have some success and feel secure. So I'll ask them easy questions to start, perhaps questions that deal more with lifestyle and feelings than with technical things. I want the players to settle into the role, to play, and I try to give them a few minutes to get used to and enjoy their time in the spotlight. Often the expert panel will interact with each other during the activity, and that's wonderful to see unless one is merely trying to steal attention from another, which very rarely happens.

When we're done, I'll ask the players how they did. Usually they'll report that they did okay, even when they excelled, either because they're modest or because they just don't know. Sometimes the performances simply aren't that good, and that's okay because this is a class, not an audition or a show, and doing is more important than excelling.

Then I'll ask the audience how the players did, and they'll usually applaud and say the players were great. There might be some charity in this, but I think most audiences really are amazed watching this game because they're on the outside of it rather than the inside and thus unaware of the players' discomfort or missteps. And maybe audience members are simply glad they weren't the ones onstage.

Sometimes I'm astounded by the players' performances. They can be funny, weird, scary, transformative, and any number of other remarkable things. This is almost always the result of players getting deeply into the role. Rather than struggling to find what their characters would say, the players seem to act as conduits for their characters' words.

When the performances don't go so well, it's often the result of players' trying too hard to be funny. They'll only be looking for the next joke rather than happening upon the humor organically as they explore their characters. Other players just can't get comfortable pretending to be an expert about something when they know nothing about it. One way or another, it's good to ask players to discuss their challenges and successes because they can be illuminating for other participants and also provide an opportunity for the leader to offer some relevant coaching.

I always try to point out when players have stayed engaged even when they haven't been in the spotlight. This not only makes their performance better but also supports the performances of the other players. Seeing a character react to something another character says or does is as engaging in scripted or improvised theater as it is in group presentations. It subtly instructs the audience to pay attention, whereas a disengaged co-performer or co-presenter diffuses attention. Sometimes I'll say that remaining engaged when one isn't in the spotlight is the equivalent of moving without the ball in basketball or soccer, and that can help nail the concept.

When we process the exercise, I ask the players if my original directions (pay attention to what you're doing with your body, breathe, and commit) were helpful. Players find most useful the instruction to be physically aware and deliberate. Often a player will say that when they didn't know what to say or do in the game, they fell back on focusing on the character's physical presence.

This is what I call a physical touchstone for an actor. When you lose the feeling of a character you still have *something*—a way of holding your head or chest or belly, walking, a vocal tone, a gesture—that helps you find that character again. You literally embody the character, and, when you get it physically, that helps you get it intellectually and emotionally. In improv or scripted work, this not only helps you find the character but also gives the character integrity and consistency.

For those of you who know or care, this is essentially the opposite of Method acting, wherein you're focused on the internal, the backstory and emotional memory of a character and trust that your exterior will reveal your interior.[25] I prefer the outside-in approach because I think it's clearer and more immediate. I've seen enough performances that might have been riveting for the performer but were a flatline for the audience because there was nothing to detect on the actor's exterior. Ultimately, however, I don't really care about actors' approaches as long as the approaches work. And you can actually combine both approaches.

The outside-in approach to character is also known, especially outside the theater, as "Fake it 'til you make it." The idea, at least as I interpret it, is that the faking here doesn't mean you're being inauthentic and certainly not a fraud but rather that you're behaving the way you wish you felt. You're faking you at your best and trusting that by be*having* that way you'll eventually *feel* that way. Another term that relates to this phenomenon, one that doesn't employ that troublesome word "fake," is "embodiment."

Scientific research suggests but hasn't yet definitely confirmed that there are observable physiological bases to embodiment. Most famously psychologist Amy Cuddy experimented with the effects of "power posing." Her TED Talk on the subject has been viewed over 60,000,000 times.[26] Cuddy asserts, in short, that we wind up feeling the way we are behaving. We can fake it until we *are* it, she says. Cuddy's TED Talk is a powerful and moving speech, and I was delighted to find scientific affirmation of my experience and intuition when I first watched it. Unfortunately, other researchers have had difficulty replicating Cuddy's findings.[27] Perhaps she chose the wrong indicators to measure even if her assertions are essentially accurate.[28]

Other studies, however, have examined the embodiment

phenomenon enough to suggest that it has a scientifically observable basis.

Dr. Andrew Wilson and Dr. Sabrina Golonka write:

> The kind of embodied cognition we advocate is the claim that the brain, while important, is not the only resource we have available to us to generate behavior. Instead, the form of our behavior emerges from the real-time interaction between a nervous system in a body with particular capabilities and an environment that offers opportunities for behavior and information about those opportunities. The reason this is quite a radical claim is that it changes the job description for the brain; instead of having to represent knowledge about the world and using that knowledge to simply output commands, the brain is now a part of a broader system that critically involves perception and action as well. The actual solution an organism comes up with for a given task includes all these elements.[29]

Science journalist Samuel McNerny adds:

> Embodied cognition, the idea that the mind is not only connected to the body but that the body influences the mind, is one of the more counter-intuitive ideas in cognitive science. In sharp contrast is dualism, a theory of mind famously put forth by René Descartes in the 17th century when he claimed that "there is a great difference between mind and body, inasmuch as body is by nature always divisible, and the mind is entirely indivisible ... the mind or soul of man is entirely different from the body" In the proceeding centuries, the notion of the disembodied mind flourished. From it, western thought developed two basic ideas: reason is disembodied because the mind is disembodied and reason is transcendent and universal. However, as George Lakoff and Rafael Núñez explain: "Cognitive science calls this entire philosophical worldview into serious question on empirical grounds... [the mind] arises from the nature of our brains, bodies, and bodily experiences. This is not just the innocuous and obvious claim that we need a body to reason; rather, it is the striking claim that the very structure of reason itself comes from the details of our embodiment.... Thus, to understand reason we must understand the details of our visual system, our motor system, and the general mechanism of neural binding."[30]

Perhaps cognitive scientist Guy Claxton put it best when he says that the brain coordinates information, but it is the "servant, not master of the body."[31]

I quote these scientists because I feel our brains are greatly resistant to the notion that they're not running the show. And indeed it is our brains that demand we get into our heads when the going gets rough rather than keeping them in their proper role as servants to our entire beings.

Underlying all of this is a long-standing mind-body dualism in western thought to which Lakoff and Núñez referred to above. Descartes of "I think, therefore I am" fame was a principal figure in articulating the notion that the mind and the body are separate and, moreover, that the mind has dominion over the body. "I think, therefore I am" seems to suggest that our thoughts would exist even if their corporeal vessels did not.

Pair Cartesian dualism with millennia of religious and philosophical thought that presents the body as base and the mind—and even more so the ineffable soul—as exalted, and you can see why we might dismiss the notion that our bodies have a say in the big picture. Perhaps accepting that what affects the body affects our intellect and emotions is easier than accepting that voluntary movement of the body can affect our thoughts and feelings.

I don't believe that the mind is predominant over the body or vice versa. Rather, I believe that we're complicated beings affected by many factors. If you've ever felt "hangry," the rage fueled by a need to eat, then you know just what I'm talking about.

As we discuss the mind and the body, I'd like to home in on the brain. Specifically, I'd like to address mirror neurons, a phenomenon that provides a physiological underpinning for much human and even primate behavior, from learning to social interaction and beyond.[32]

Neurological experiments have revealed that we have subconscious responses in our brains that make us feel we're actually experiencing what others are doing, even though we're only observing them. In brain scans the same areas that "light up" when we do something are also activated when we only watch someone else do it. Your body's involuntary reactions to things like film and sporting events point to this. Ever "help" someone on TV make a free throw or cringe when a character in a movie has a really awkward moment? That's what I'm talking about here.

The ramifications for presenters and performers are enormous. Mirror neurons are at the heart of empathy and contagious emotional and physical reactions. Your audience feels deeply and partially subconsciously what you present to them. So as your behavior affects you, so it affects your audience. Duh, right? But this goes deep.

People can't see or hear your feelings; they can only see and hear your behavior. If you behave in a way that exudes confidence and authority, it follows that your audience will respond to you as though you truly have those qualities. Their mirror neurons along with their more conscious processes will engender this response.

If your audience is responding to you as though you are authoritative, then your mirror neurons are going to start flaring and your conscious responses are going to add to that effect, and you'll start to feel the way you hoped to feel. Then the audience will pick up on your increased confidence and feel better about you, which in turn affects you. It's a virtuous cycle and gives us a scientific basis for the somewhat glib "fake it 'til you make it."

The opposite is having a presence that says, "I don't belong here." Behave in unconfident fashion, and your audience will pick up on it and start to think and feel that you're not authoritative and that you're an impostor. And how's that going to make you feel? Worse. That makes your audience feel worse, and now you're in a tailspin.

Now I can't promise you that every situation will go exactly as I've just described it. I've failed when I used my best technique and succeeded when I've been sloppy. However, I think being aware of these phenomena and trusting them is the surest approach.

It's also important to remember that, outside of anxiety dreams, if you're asked to present some expertise, it's not by accident. Your knowledge might be highly specialized. Or maybe everyone in your audience knows you're a novice, and they don't expect you to know everything. Maybe your audience is even *supposed* to challenge you, for instance in a dissertation defense. You might need to remind yourself that you belong where you are and that you know what you're talking about. A physical reminder, some small talisman but not necessarily a tattoo on the back of your hand, can reinforce this message to yourself.

That what you say is not as important as how you say it might be a sad or even dangerous truth. It's obviously ethically slippery. Good liars usually present their fictions well. There's not much I can do about that except to say that I'm not encouraging people to lie. Dishonesty is not a good or sustainable practice. But, hey, the Force can be used for good or evil, and that's pretty much your choice and your consequences to live.

I don't think you have to lie anyway. Even a confident, authoritative, and well-prepared person can't be expected to know everything. You can say, "I don't know," without losing your authority (just not in Expert Interview). As a person in power, I say that rather often and use it as an opportunity to start dialogue. A student might ask a question I can't answer, and I'll respond, "I don't know. That's a good question. What do you think?"

If you're the person without the power in a situation, you might reply, "I'm not prepared to answer that question, but I can find out and get back to you, or I can think out loud and share my reasoning with you." You might have turned a losing situation into one in which you can impress your audience with your resilience, resourcefulness, and thought process. By the way, most interviewers are looking for interviewees to display such skills. I also suspect most potential clients are more impressed with honest interaction than glossy bullshit.

Put another way, being an infallible robot might not be as attractive as being a trustworthy human being. Naturally, there are some people who aren't going to be satisfied with anything less than perfection. I can't tell you what to do in such cases, but I can say that I would simply rather not work with or for someone who's that unreasonable. I've found out the hard way that some jobs, clients, bosses, friends, and romantic partners just aren't worth having. Detaching yourself from a toxic situation might be difficult, but if it preserves your dignity and well-being, then that's an authoritative move, even if it doesn't always feel like one.

Years ago one of my Duke undergrads wanted to talk to me after class. He was about to graduate and had set up exactly one interview. Naturally he was very anxious about it. So I asked him how he was preparing. He said he was studying every possible question he could imagine being asked in the company's field. When I asked him if he thought he could foresee every potential query, he admitted he couldn't.

"Would you say that your knowledge base is where it should be, given that you're leaving college for this professional situation?" I asked.

He replied in the affirmative.

"Given that you'll be interviewing for an entry-level position and meeting with experts in the field, isn't it safe to say that you'll probably know the least of anyone in the room?"

Another yes.

"But if you know what you should know, perhaps your interviewers will be more interested in the way you present yourself, your self-possession and likeability, and your ability to think." I added that some research, particularly on the specific company, was a good idea but that it was clear he was just making himself feel uptight and insufficient when he could instead be feeling relaxed and qualified.

Well, he got the job. I think I coached him well, although he's the guy who did all the work. He was successful, I believe, because he accepted the reality of his situation, found confidence in that, and then performed with authority befitting his position. He wasn't an impostor, and he didn't act like one. All that said, I think it's also good not to bet everything you have on a single hand.

Present your expertise, whatever it is, so that it's believable for your audience and so they trust and respect you. Don't undercut your message, present it strongly. In my experience, the trouble people run into when presenting is not that they don't know the material, it's that they present it weakly as if they didn't know it, and that can be a pretty big problem.

Exercises

Individual

1. **Happy Systems Check**
    A. The next time you're around people or in a situation that makes you happy and confident, notice the way you're holding your body and how it feels.
    B. Next, try to recreate those positions and feelings in situations where there are no external stimuli actively making you feel good. Perhaps you're waiting for a bus or a coffee or just walking down the hall at work or school. Try on confident and happy. People might even ask you what's up.
    C. Act happy and confident in more challenging situations. Increasing the level of difficulty can help make this positive response second nature. Just don't choose a pressure-packed moment to start practicing; it won't do you much good then.
2. Watch the Cuddy video.
3. Walk around your home pretending to be a superhero. If you don't like that kind of fiction, you can try some other approach, perhaps world leader, cowpoke, movie star, or professional wrestler. Take up space, and make some noise too!

4. Practice speaking in a mirror. Your speech might be scripted, planned, or impromptu. Try to exaggerate your authority and power at first. Notice how it feels. Modulate your approach, and notice how that looks and feels. You need to experiment to find what works for you.

Group

1. **Expert Interview Demonstration** (good for in-person or virtual groups)
    A. Ask for three volunteers to play the role of guests on your talk show. Tell them they'll be experts in a field assigned to them by the audience and that they shouldn't know much about it. Before you get the suggestions, instruct the volunteers to focus on physicality, breathing, and commitment during the activity.
    B. Solicit areas of expertise or occupations from your audience. If you feel a suggestion might be controversial, ask the volunteer if they're comfortable with it. Some volunteers would be delighted to play an exotic dancer, others not so much.
    C. Interview the experts one by one. Ask them several questions. Leading questions are good. If they're struggling, try to help them.
    D. Ask the audience to ask questions of the experts.
    E. Wrap up the game by having the experts share their mottos.
    F. Wave your imaginary magic wand, and tell the players that the game is over and they're back to their normal selves. Ask them how they did.
    G. Ask the audience how they thought the volunteers did.
    H. Discuss challenges, successes, and real-world relevance.
2. **Expert Interview All Play** (good for in-person or virtual groups)
    Expert Interview is such an important activity that I want to make sure everyone in class gets a chance to play. If your group is fewer than ten people, you can repeat the game a couple times, perhaps getting a student to play the role of host.
    A. If your group numbers ten or more, create breakout

groups of five to ten. Subdivide the breakouts into groups of two to four. So if you have a breakout of ten, you might have a panel of six interviewers questioning a panel of four experts. Or if it's a breakout of only five, you might have three interviewing two.

B. Explain that you'll start with one subgroup in each breakout playing experts. Everyone else in the group gives the experts their specialties and interviews them.

C. As the breakout groups are playing, watch how it's going, if only because it will help you to know when it's time to finish each subgroup's time in the spotlight. You might also drop in and ask a question.

D. Tell the breakouts to ask their experts for their mottos, and tell the experts to remember their own mottos.

E. Rotate to the next subgroup in each breakout, and repeat the game until everyone has had a chance to play expert.

F. Once everyone has played, get the entire group back together.

G. If you're in a virtual environment, have each participant state their motto in character.

H. If you're in person, you can have each participant walk in character in front of the entire group, stop, and state their motto. You can do this while participants are standing in a circle or in one or two lines.

I. Ask the participants how the activity went for them.

14

Movement and Meaning

"All that is important is this one moment in movement.
Make the moment important, vital, and worth living.
Do not let it slip away unnoticed and unused."
—Martha Graham

Onstage or screen, movement is enormously important. Not only does it help to tell the story, but it also helps us understand the characters. An example that springs to mind immediately for me is the opening sequence from *Saturday Night Fever*.[33] John Travolta's character is shown walking down a Brooklyn street, and just by his walk and the way he surveys his surroundings, we get a sense of who this guy is. The juxtaposition of the walk and wardrobe with his carrying a can of paint and stuffing a slice of pizza in his mouth gives the character complexity. The audience knows a lot about the character before he even says anything.

Another example, much shorter from the small screen, can be seen in the opening credits of *Mary Tyler Moore* in the show's later years (not to be confused with the series' original opening).[34] Mary is walking along a path beside Lake of the Isles in Minneapolis. Her stride is long, her arms are swinging, and her head is up. She even checks out a couple of male runners (played by series co-creator James L. Brooks and producer David Davis) as they pass. What does the audience glean from this brief shot? This is a confident, self-possessed woman. She's wholesome in that she's exercising in a natural setting, but she's not naïve, which we see by her taking notice of the runners. And is she returning a greeting to them or checking out their asses? More mystery and texture....

These are two obvious examples, and I cite them because they stuck in my developing brain when I first saw them but also because you can easily find them online. As crucial as movement is onscreen, it is equally or even more so onstage. Notice movement in a play, dance concert, or improv show, and you'll quickly realize what a big effect it has on the production. This is also true of speeches and presentations.

When I'm directing improv or scripted work for the stage, I pay great attention to the players' movements. In scripted pieces, I want movement to jibe with the characters as they're written and as we've interpreted them for the production. If the movement doesn't match the words, that's okay as long as it's deliberate. We want the characters to have integrity, for them to be cohesive and make sense to the audience.

In improv we don't have a script, but often we'll discover a character just by the way we move. (Indeed I've included an exercise at the end of this chapter on that very thing.) Often I've started onstage in an improv show with little or no idea about my character only to find I have a pretty clear idea by the time I arrive simply based on the way I'm carrying myself.

Movement onstage is something you can explore in many ways through books and classes. And you've probably already figured out that if movement is important onstage, it's also important in everyday life. In fact, that's *why* movement is important onstage—art imitates life. Even if you're not a stage actor you stand to benefit from increasing your awareness of movement, gaining control over it, and realizing its effects on you and others.

One way I approach this topic is with an exercise I simply call "Walking." We find an open area, perhaps a big empty room, a foyer, or a courtyard, and, no surprise, walk. I split the group into two and have the subsections line up at opposite ends of the space where they're walking. They walk toward and past each other as they cross the space. If space is very tight, I have them walk in flights, one after the other. Before the walking starts, I instruct participants to let their hands swing freely at their sides and to keep their eyes up so they can see where they're going and I can see their eyes. We will refer to this way of walking as "normal." I encourage students to notice the way their body feels as they're walking.

By the way, people in wheelchairs can participate in this exercise. I'm not an expert in that kind of movement, but I imagine that much of the direction for people on their feet in this exercise also applies to those in chairs.

After they cross the space a couple times, I'll ask participants what part of their bodies they feel they're leading with. In other words, if they were to walk into a wall, what part of their bodies, excluding arms and legs, would hit the wall first? Or maybe it's easier for them to imagine what part of their body, between the top of their head and the bottom of their torso, is pulling them through space.

It might be the nose or the chest or the hips or just about anything. Scientific precision doesn't matter here because we're simply trying to increase awareness and perhaps think about movement in a way different from how we normally do. So each player walks leading with whatever part seems right to them.

Next I'll ask participants to focus on the lead part and exaggerate their walk based on that. So perhaps a player is jutting out their chin just a bit. I should be able to tell what part is leading, as should other participants. After one or two passes, I'll ask players to exaggerate even more to what I call "Clown Level," meaning that they could be performing in a circus or huge theater, and audiences could still recognize them as the Chin Clown or the Belly Clown. (It's worth noting that, in my experience, pretty much everyone born after 1975 hates clowns and finds them scary. Yet there seems to be no issue if they're asked to behave clownishly and the instruction is meant to suggest being very demonstrative and silly.)

The parade continues as the walkers cross the space leading with the same part that I call out. I might instruct them to walk leading with hips, then make another cross leading with forehead, then chest, neck, and so on. I also call out variations in intensity among regular, exaggerated, and clown levels. The goal here is for participants to gain awareness of how leading with varying parts of the body feels. As the participants walk, I often call out coaching, almost always encouragement, usually to those who are doing very well, so that others can see what's possible and permissible, and to those who are struggling so that they feel supported and like they're making progress. Sometimes I'll call out the "normal" direction as a palette cleanser.

After everyone has made ten to 15 crosses, I'll stop and let the group decompress. There's usually some laughter and excited chatter. Once they've settled down, I'll ask the participants how the exercise is going for them and what they've observed in themselves and others. Generally I'll hear that walking in certain ways led to certain feelings. Perhaps, for example, leading with the chest engenders confidence or leading with the neck leads to feelings of vulnerability. Often a player will comment on how leading with one part of the body necessitates an adjustment somewhere else in the body, especially in exaggerated versions. Some participants might mention an approach they really liked or disliked, and this is a good question to ask reticent groups.

I refer to this first step of the exercise, leading with various body parts, as establishing physical vocabulary. Players should now understand different ways of moving and how they feel and have specific names for what they're doing. This is important because the next iteration of the exercise focuses on the director's calling out emotional or mental states for the participants to embody while walking. Most of us already have an idea of how to express emotions through our walks, but the physical vocabulary helps deconstruct how we do it.

We now begin the second part of the exercise. The emotional states I call out for the group depend upon the group's composition and my own mood and inspiration. Regardless, I like to start simply, so I might start with suggestions like being happy or sad, intelligent, or stupid. And again I'll use three intensity levels: regular, exaggerated, and clown. As the players get more repetitions, they tend to get more comfortable and develop more control. Therefore, I like to challenge them with increasingly complex suggestions.

"You've just received a text from someone you really like on the opposite side of the room, and they've just confessed they're in love with you."

"You're walking toward an office building with a lot of windows for an interview you know you're going to ace. You want anyone looking out the windows to see your confidence."

"Someone on the other side of the room has just suffered a terrible loss, and you're going to comfort them."

"You're rushing to class or work and you know you've forgotten something, but you can't remember what."

Coming up with scenarios is fun for me, and usually I'll ask for the participants to suggest some. While some of your suggestions should focus on "useful" emotions like confidence or empathy, working with *any* emotion helps to develop physical awareness, control, and expressiveness. I've never counted the number of suggestions I give or passes the players make in this part of the exercise, but I suspect it's around 20. When energy starts to flag, it's time to wrap up the exercise.

When you're done walking, get everyone seated together to discuss what you've just done. After all that walking and adapting, most people will be very eager to talk about what they experienced and what the applications are. They might mention what they saw others doing, and, of course, the leader should share observations as well.

I find I have very little lecturing to do after this exercise, but I still have a few exhortations for my groups. One is to be aware that in the real world "the show" starts the moment other people can see you and maybe even beforehand. That means be at your best before you enter the room where you'll be performing, whether it's a presentation, interview, or meeting. I've actually seen presenters slouch into a room and then change their character once they reach the podium. Now they're composed and enthusiastic, but I wonder what happened to the schlub who first walked into the room.

Another practice I want to encourage is experimentation. Yes, we have our default walks, but at some point in our lives we chose, consciously or subconsciously, our normal way of moving. Is this way the best way for us? You might have poor posture, an ungainly gait, or a tendency to look down or up. Idiosyncrasies are fine, and I'm not suggesting we all walk the same "correct" way. However I do feel we should strive to move purposefully and gracefully.

As you experiment with your walk, you might well find that your mood is affected.[35] We examined the science behind this in the previous chapter. Walk like a happy person, with your arms swinging, your head up, and a spring in your step, and you'll probably feel happy—and appear happy to other people. (You're free to substitute, "confident," "capable," "sexy," or something else for "happy" here.) Walk like a sad person, arms at your sides, gaze down, and shuffling, and you'll probably feel sad and look sad to others.

Now I don't mean to suggest that all is lost if you have an impairment that keeps you from walking peppy any more than I'd suggest that you can't convey power or confidence if you're short or have a high voice. I'd rather suggest that you explore your potential and limitations and see what feels best. And let me stress that this is for *you* and not only about how others perceive you.

Another movement activity I use is one I call Greet and Growl. It's really a suite of at least two exercises that I've combined into one. It's kinda weird, so I don't start a course or program with this and only trot it out when a group has some experience and are comfortable with each other. I've been told that my introduction to the activity is overly scary, but I'd rather have people overprepared than underprepared.

I announce that the exercise will take about 15 minutes and that at some point almost everyone will be out of their comfort zone. But I emphasize that, in that case, most everyone will be thinking of themselves and not others. I add that when players start to feel uncomfortable, they should strive to enter the FIZ by understanding the stakes and focusing on what they're doing rather than their discomfort and others' possible reactions. After all, if you can't do something silly and meaningless, how can you possibly expect to do something serious and meaningful? Finally, I reiterate something that I say early in my courses: focus on what you're doing now, and we'll discuss meaning later; by searching for meaning, you might miss the meaning inherent in the experience.

In a room clear of furniture with plenty of space to move, I have participants walk through the space with arms swinging freely and heads up, eyes at eye-contact level. Starting with the "normal" walk allows us to be clear about how we're adjusting during the exercise. I instruct students to move from point to point in the room with deliberation rather than falling into zombie-like laps.

I also direct the participants to remain aware of how they're carrying their bodies and that this awareness should extend to how their movement makes them feel. "Take a ride in your body," one of my instructors once told me, meaning I should be cognizant of the way I'm propelling myself, what I'm leading with, where I might be holding tension, and so forth.

As the participants walk around the room, I tell them that when I say "go," they'll approach other players and introduce themselves to each other by shaking hands and making the following exchange: "Hello, I'm [Player One's name]," "Hello, I'm [Player Two's name]." Then they'll move on to the next person and reintroduce themselves. This continues even if the players encounter someone a second or third time.

Once I see that everyone seems to have introduced themselves to each other, I call out, "Back to normal." Then I instruct the participants to reflect on their interactions as they continue to walk. How did they shake hands? Where did they look? How did they speak?

Now I tell the walkers that when I say "go," we'll repeat the introductions, only the participants will exaggerate their behavior from the first round of introductions. Go. This is usually pretty comical.

People surprise me with how well they can satirize themselves, and they seem to enjoy it as well.

Back to normal walking after this second round of introductions, I ask the participants to reflect on their exaggerated behavior. I tell them I'm going to ask them to make an intuitive leap. If they were to exaggerate their behavior so far that their character turned into an animal, what would that animal be? "The first animal that springs to mind is the right answer," I say, adding, "If nothing has come to mind yet, then just pick something because when I say 'go,' I want you to interact with each other as those animals. Go!"

Bedlam. As with Walking, I try to encourage people. The bolder players will crawl on the ground and jump in the air, and I make a point of praising that and saying, "That is what's permitted." Some participants will be more restrained, but, when I see them going for it, I'll laud that. My goal here is to make everyone feel good about and comfortable with the craziness and also to have the more ambitious students lead by example. Commitment to the exercise is contagious—as is lack of commitment.

"Back to normal," I instruct after the interactions. "As you're moving through the space, I'd like you to find an object in the room, stop, and look at it, keeping in mind that people aren't objects." Once everyone has found an object, and I might have to coach them into looking at something specific, I continue. "Look at this object without thinking about its name or use. Try to see it as if you've never seen it before. See it like a baby might see it, as just shape and color. If it has letters or numbers on it, just see them as shapes. Try to see it until it stops making sense."

I have the participants look at their objects for at least 60 seconds. They'll begin to get restless, and a little bit of that is okay, but I don't want to torture them. After that minute I say, "Once you've seen the object, let it see you, whatever that means and it might not mean anything at all." This might provoke some laughter, and that's okay too. If some people are feeling transcendent, that's great, but I want those who don't to feel accepted as well. Laughter can arise for many different reasons, but I think it's generally good and indicates that people are playing and having a reasonably good time, even if they're challenged and confused, so I try to keep a light touch.

After a total of about two minutes focusing on objects, I call out, "Back to normal." As the players move around the room, I say, "I'm about to ask you to make another intuitive leap. A moment ago you were moving around the room as animals. Now I'd like you to think of that animal and what its opposite is. Obviously this is not a scientific question, so just follow what your gut tells you. And pick something now because when I say 'go' I want you once again to interact with the other animals in the room. Go!"

And they're off once again. Usually the players' willingness to throw themselves into their portrayals increases. In fact we're generally making quite a racket at this point. Often I'll see shy people pacing and roaring as lions or dominant people scurrying and squeaking as mice. I call out encouragement as I see fit, and once everyone seems to have interacted with everyone else, I call out, "Back to normal." Then I repeat the exercise in which participants focus on objects (different objects from the first iteration) and have the objects "see" them.

Back to normal we go. I tell the players that we're nearing the end of the exercise, adding, "You've now played two animals, one that grew out of an exaggeration of your own behavior and one that is the opposite of that. Now I want you to think of an *ideal* animal, one that really speaks to you, one that might be on your family crest if you had one. Maybe it's not even a real animal or an animal at all, but whatever it is, I want you to interact with each other as that ideal being. Go!"

This part of the exercise is beautiful to me. Most everyone will be standing or striding proudly, gliding or soaring. Their heads are held high, their eyes calmly and confidently surveying their surroundings and taking in the other players.

After what seems the suitable amount of time, I return the group back to normal. "Now we're going to go back to where we started. You're going to introduce yourselves to each other, and you're simply going to be yourselves again. Only I want you to have a secret, and that secret is that you are your ideal being. If that's an eagle, don't *act* like an eagle; just know that you *are* an eagle deep down inside. Go."

The participants interact, and it's always stunningly different from their first round of introductions in this exercise. There seems to be a quiet energy in the room, gravitas where there was originally nervous chatter. The players seem to pay more attention to each other, really see and hear, and take time with each other. They seem to enjoy these introductions.

Once the introductions are complete, I have the participants go back to normal for just a moment, and then I instruct them to come to a relaxed stop (not a freeze). I have them take in a couple of deep breaths and release them with a sigh. And then I have them grab a chair, and we return to a circle to process the exercise.

I have all sorts of questions for them.

- How did that go for you?
- Did I build it up too big, not enough, or just right? (Usually players will say I built it up too much, almost scoffing at how much easier it was than I made it seem. I do this intentionally because I think that if you warn people something's going to be *really* weird, then just about anything you do won't be that weird because the participants' imaginations will have run wild. They keep waiting for it to get truly bizarre, but that moment never comes, and then the exercise is over and they're relieved.)
- Did you observe a difference in the room at the end of the exercise compared to the beginning?
- What did you observe?
- What was challenging?
- What's useful?

Let people talk and *listen*. You might have some observations or experience you'd like to contribute. The most important thing is to let the people who just engaged in the exercise discuss what they experienced and observed.

Participants tend to be excited about the exercise because moving in a deliberate, ideal way inspires them and makes them feel happy. There's been plenty of research about visualization and its effects on performance.[36] Well here's a chance not only to visualize but also to experiment with what you're visualizing.

This exercise is related to Expert Interview in that it gives one a chance to find a physical "home base" or touchstone. I've even heard people say their ideal being felt like a protective shield, even when they weren't obviously portraying that animal. Another way of putting this might be to say to yourself, "It's okay. I got this. I'm a dragon [or whatever the ideal being is]."

Players always wonder about the part of the exercise where they're just looking at objects and then imagining the objects looking back at them. So I'll ask them why they thought we did it. Their responses can be mundane, sublime, or somewhere in the middle. I've heard comments like, "As I tried to imagine how the object saw me, I felt I was able to gain greater self-awareness," or, "I became aware that the object is a manifestation of the divine." Hearing others' perspectives keeps things fresh for me.

My reasons for including the object meditation in Greet and Growl are varied. It provides a physical rest and a chance for quiet inward reflection between periods of energetic and even chaotic outward exertion. I also feel that focusing on the object is another chance to practice Paul Sills' "see what you see, not what you *think* you see," a perspective that can be very helpful in problem-solving. Often a problem becomes obscured by our emotional or intellectual reaction to the extent that we eventually no longer see the real issue at all.

Greet and Growl in many ways is just a more extreme example of Walking, and sometimes one will work for a student better than the other. I'll admit that I get a little nervous about Greet and Growl because it's pretty unconventional. However I don't have a group do either exercise until I feel the group is ready for it. I also continue to get powerfully positive feedback about both activities, and that tells me they're worth doing. Each provides an opportunity for participants to push themselves and to get out of and expand their comfort zones.

Both Walking and Greet and Growl are about developing physical awareness, being physically deliberate, and solving the challenge of expressing a thought, emotion, or identity nonverbally through movement. We already convey information to ourselves and others through our movement; why not be aware and in control of the process?

Exercises

Individual

1. Go for a walk. Instead of concentrating on where you're going, think about *how* you're going. Pay attention to how your body feels. Is anything painful, tense, or out of balance? If so, can you adjust your walk to remedy that? What feels good? What is the source of the power that moves you through space?

2. Deliberately play and experiment with walking. Try leading with different parts of your body (e.g., nose, chest, hips). Try

embodying different emotions. Try a walking impression of different characters or character types (cowboy, shy nerd, sex bomb). You might have to make adjustments to get it to feel right, and you don't have to do this in public. You might find, however, that some of the walks feel pretty good and improve your mood and/or confidence level, in which case you should definitely try them out in public.

3. As you go through your day and interact with people, reflect on your behavior and imagine what animal it's most like. Then think about what kind of animal you'd like to embody. It could be a bear or a bunny or a Komodo dragon; it's all up to you. Pretend to be that animal in private, just like you might have played as a child. Perhaps you'll want to try on a couple of other animals for size while you're at it. Then try secretly embodying this ideal being in your interactions with other people. It should be subtle, strong enough so that you're aware of it but not so strong that you're freaking out yourself or other people. And yes, it sounds strange, but this is the kind of thing we all did regularly as kids until we grew up, quit having fun, and stopped learning.

Group

Sorry, I can't imagine how either of these can work online, but perhaps there's a facial expression exercise waiting to be invented for that format.[37]

1. **Walking**

Below is the basic outline, while a detailed description is above.

A. Find an area that takes at least five seconds to walk across. Participants should have the opportunity to get into stride. If your group is small enough, they can all walk across at the same time. If it's too big for that, you can have half the group at one end and half at the other and have them walk toward and pass each other as they cross the space, or they can walk in the same direction in smaller subgroups.

B. Participants walk "normally," with arms swinging freely, and gaze up. They should figure out what part of their bodies, aside from legs and arms, is leading.

C. Participants explore leading with different parts of the

body. How does leading with different parts change the way they feel? What adjustments are necessary?

    D. Check in with your group to see how they're doing.

    E. Now the director gives emotions or states of mind to convey with walking. Having tried leading with different parts of the body, players should have a sense of the interconnectedness of body parts and their technique as they embody the directions. If the participants aren't being obvious enough, have them try at higher degrees of intensity, like the clown level. (Once you have established what exaggeration looks and feels like, it's much easier to be subtle.)

    F. Discuss.

2. **Greet and Growl**

    A. Have the group move through the room "normally," arms swinging freely and gazes up. Emphasize awareness, first of self and then of others.

    B. Introductions: Handshake and "Hello, I'm...."

    C. Back to normal walking.

    D. Introductions based on self-exaggeration.

    E. Back to normal walking, imagining what animal one's behavior would become if it were exaggerated to an extreme extent.

    F. Be that animal and interact with others.

    G. Back to normal walking.

    H. Find an object to look at, and try to see it truly without imposing projections or interpretations. After 60 seconds, let the object see you for another minute.

    I. Back to normal walking, thinking about what animal is the opposite of the first animal you were.

    J. Be that second animal, and interact with others.

    K. Back to normal walking.

    L. Find a second object to look at, and try to see it truly without imposing projections or interpretations. After 60 seconds, let the object see you for another minute.

    M. Back to normal walking, imagining an ideal animal or being for oneself.

    N. Be that third animal or being, and interact with others.

    O. Back to normal walking.

P. Introductions: Handshake and "Hello, I'm…" but channeling without acting like ideal beings.
Q. Back to normal walking.
R. Come to a relaxed standing stop.
S. Sit down and discuss.

15

Behavioral Status

The Bunny and the Bear

"In everything, therefore, treat people the same way you want them to treat you." [38]—St. Matthew

Behavioral status isn't power; it's the *appearance* of power. At least that's how I'm defining it here. High behavioral status looks like high power or domination, and low behavioral status looks like low power or submission.

Comedies and dramas onstage and screen are filled with status play and manipulation because status is a significant part of everyday life. You can observe status in action whenever two or more people interact. Sometimes it's obvious and sometimes it's subtle.

Behavioral status is powerful because it's so primal. You can observe status projection in the animal world, and the methods animals use to express domination or submission are very similar to those people use. We are, after all, animals too.

Status can be very useful in animal populations because it allows hierarchies and power struggles to occur without necessitating violence. If a group of animals is spilling a lot of blood just trying to figure out its social order, its chances of survival diminish. So animals pose and roar and dance and work things out that way. It's almost like animal theater. Of course, sometimes displays of status are not enough to resolve the situation, and violence ensues.

I've already mentioned positions of power in the chapter on acting authoritatively. They really should be called "positions of status" because no matter how much space you take up, your literal power isn't likely to change. However you might appear and feel more powerful, and that's status.

Regardless of how we label them, demonstrations of high status or domination are essentially about taking up space. You make your body appear bigger, perhaps by puffing out your chest and/or crossing your arms. Picture a superhero or a bouncer; their physical posture conveys power and even potential violence. Nonhuman animals are also good at taking up space when they're trying to show themselves as a formidable foe or attractive mate, and they often have fur, feathers, and fins to help make themselves appear even more imposing and impressive. Picture a dog's hackles, a peacock's feathers, or a cobra's hood.

Taking up space might often mean not only taking up neutral territory but also taking someone else's territory. If someone gets in your face or is invading your space in some other way, that's an assertion of dominance. There are exceptions to this rule, like kissing (in most cases), but as I'll discuss later, the same behavior can be an assertion of high or low status, the determining factor being the context.

You can take up audial space as well by being loud. Humans and other animals often roar to assert high status. Quality of sound can also convey high status; think about the very low-pitched voices we often hear announcers use when the message is supposed to sound important. A steady voice can suggest high status.

Animals even use scent to convey high status, often marking their territory with it. I suppose people do this too, although I'm not always certain how intentional it is. I have heard of athletes trying to intimidate opponents with bad breath or bodily funkiness, but this is rare and not that relevant to this discussion. Still, I would say that it behooves us to be aware of the way we smell because odor can affect others primally. It's best to avoid overwhelming amounts of perfume or cologne or walking around with casseroles in your armpits.

Demonstrations of low status and submission are basically the opposite of high-status behavior. Most simply it's about taking up less space and being quieter. You make your body smaller. You slump and shrink and wrap yourself in knots. You use higher or unsteady tones.

You probably already get the picture, but it might help to think about how dogs display status. When submitting to each other and to people, dogs not only make themselves small, but they often get on the ground, show their bellies, and whimper. This is in contrast to high-status displays of standing tall, baring their teeth, and growling or barking. Even their eyes look different depending on what status they're trying to convey.

So far we've discussed behavioral status at its most basic level. Not surprisingly, I refer to this as "animal status." I like to go one step further by calling high animal status "Bear" and low animal status "Bunny." Those might not be the best examples, but pretty much everyone knows what you mean when you direct them to act like a bear or a bunny.

We can talk all we like about behavioral status, but probably the best way to understand and start to master it is to get on our feet and explore what it looks, sounds, and feels like. In his book *Impro*,[39] Keith Johnstone has a wonderful status exercise, "Sir/Smith." The scene is a boss firing an employee. Provided you stick to the script, which serves as the control in this experiment, that low-power employee is always going to get fired by that high-power boss. (I've adapted the script, renamed it "Boss/Smith," and included it at chapter's end.)

The delightful challenge of the exercise is finding ways to manipulate each character's status to see how different the scene can be even while having the same words. So let's say the boss wilts in his chair, looks at his feet, and stutters while the employee leans back in her chair and laughs condescendingly at everything the boss says. This is reverse status, meaning high power is the Bunny while low power is the Bear. The boss still has the power, but the employee has the higher status, and sometimes status can be so high that it trumps power.

There are other status manipulations you can use in this scene. There's the status shift, wherein the director calls out "switch," and the character that had high status now has low and vice versa. If done at a dramatic point in the script, it heightens the effect. You can have a status "tower" in which each player must top the status displayed in the other player's previous line. The opposite is the status "tunnel," in which each player vies for subsequently decreasing status.

When you work with status, most players will already have ideas about how to play high and low because it's something they do and see every day. That said, you can help your players by giving or having the audience give them three high- or low-status behaviors they can use. Focus on posture, movement, voice, manners of speech, tempo, eye contact, and spatial relationship. There's so much to explore that I never tire of this exercise even after decades of playing it.

Coach the players to go big (but short of actual interpersonal violence). Emphasize that the exercise is not about subtlety or social convention. We want them to see what they're capable of before they start modulating their performances. At the end of the scene, ask the players if they could have taken their status further. They'll usually answer yes, and then I usually ask them why they didn't. I might seem a bit like a drill sergeant or a football coach doing that, but my goal is to get the players out of their comfort zones. Naturally, you can push your players while still being positive, polite, and friendly.

When playing Boss/Smith, give as many participants as you can the chance to play, and ask the audience what they observe. What works? What's interesting? What's funny? What's uncomfortable?

You might well find yourself discussing context because high-status behavior in one situation might be low in another, or opposite behaviors might convey the same status. For example, looking directly at someone can express high status, as in staring someone down, but looking away can also express high status by suggesting disgust or indifference. Or with low status you can avoid eye contact, conveying that you're intimidated or ashamed, or maintain eye contact to indicate that you're desperately hanging on every word or glance. You can laugh uproariously at what someone says and thus assert high status, or you can titter nervously to come across low. A quiet voice can indicate timidity, or it can be extraordinarily powerful, a demand that others adapt to the speaker's chosen volume.

You'll probably find that there are moments when the audience sympathizes with a player using low status. Maybe the low-status player seems pitiable or the high-status player seems cruel or overbearing. This not only makes for compelling theater but also forces us to look more closely at status.

For years I taught behavioral status haunted by the realization that something was missing from my lesson. I wasn't trying to teach people to be dominators, but Boss/Smith seemed to be saying that might makes right, which isn't an enlightened concept. Maybe that sympathetic response to the "good guy" in Boss/Smith was a clue to the missing aspect.

If there's a hero and a villain in Boss/Smith, perhaps morality is a piece of the puzzle. And if we're comparing human behavior to that of animals, what differentiates us from them? After much reflection and many discussions, I reached the conclusion that there's a civil component of status to go along with the animal. If the Bear and

Bunny mark the high and low extremes of the animal-status continuum, then high civil status could be symbolized by Angel and low by
Devil. (Feel free to employ what terminology works best for you; I'm
just trying to keep it simple here. And, as an animal lover, I feel compelled to add that I'm not trying to denigrate our fauna friends, from
whom we can learn much about living well, but merely trying to use
clear illustrations.)

Civilization is based upon the idea that people have rights
regardless of their ability to defend them. You could argue that laws
are codes of conduct essentially designed to protect the physically
weak. So Bear status might work well in the wilderness but becomes
bullying, boorishness, and tyranny in the city.

Once we've explored animal status in class, I like to ask my students to suggest situations in which a person with power might use
low animal status to be effective. They usually have some great examples, and I have a few of my own to add. Common themes include
conveying empathy, developing trust, building consensus, delegating
authority, and other actions that make for a good leader.

In *Primal Leadership*, Daniel Goleman asserts that effective
people must be flexible with their behavioral status.[40] This relates
to Emotional IQ and indicates that civil status plays a bigger role in
success than does mere animal status. "Powerless communication"
is another term suggesting that, for competent people, civility and
humanity are likely to carry the day over bluster and swagger.[41]

As a teacher and director, I've found that some people respond
better to the Bunny and others respond better to the Bear—
and almost everyone responds best to something between those
extremes. Sometimes people's responses are different on different
days, and I don't always get it right. Regardless of my animal status or tactics, my goal is always to maintain high civil status, which
facilitates learning, growth, and improvement. I try to avoid low
civil status, which demeans and hurts others. It's an endless learning
experience, and, after all these years, I still don't know if I'm a hard
guy or a softie. My students and others I've led have probably called
me both (and a few other things as well).

It's worth noting that people sometimes deliberately pair low
animal status with low civil status to pursue the ends they seek. This
is called manipulation or passive aggression. This approach is low on
the civil continuum (i.e., unethical) because it's at heart dishonest or
at least not forthright. Using negative emotions, like guilt, shame, or

embarrassment, to motivate others isn't highly evolved even though it's more civilized than actual physical violence.

Incidentally, sarcasm is low civil-status behavior because it's dishonest; you're presenting as true something that isn't. Not everyone who uses sarcasm intends it negatively, but it can be harmful, communicating indifference and denigrating another's concerns. While caustic sarcasm can seem a formidable weapon, I've found it wilts if you take it at face value. Playing dumb in such instances forces an honest interaction, even if it's not necessarily a positive one.

After discussing animal status versus civil status in class, I like to have a final run-through of the Boss/Smith scene and this time have both players playing high status but with one adopting civil and the other animal. I invite the animal to use low civil status, any dirty trick in the book they can imagine, as long as no one actually gets hurt.

This high/high version of Boss/Smith is usually a lot of fun and often a bit creepy. In essence the animal is trying to drag the civil down to the animal level, and, if the animal succeeds, the animal wins. If the civil can maintain the moral high ground despite the challenges, then the civil has prevailed. Of course not all social and professional interactions are about winning and losing, and that binary perspective isn't even healthy. However, everyday phrases like "losing your temper" and "losing your head" compared to "winning someone over" and "winning someone's heart" hint at our deep societal understanding of what's at stake when animal and civil statuses are in conflict.

So how do you know if your behavior is high or low on the civil scale? Usually we have a sense of what we want from an interaction, and it's only sensible self-interest to pursue that. The means one employs and the regard for others determine the civil status of one's behavior. As naïve as it might sound, my golden rule for maintaining high civil status, regardless of the power structure, revolves around two questions: Am I treating the other(s) with dignity and respect, and am I treating myself with dignity and respect? If I can answer yes to both of these questions, then I trust I'll behave in a civil, moral fashion and will adapt my animal status appropriately.

It's my experience that the most productive interactions occur when all parties try to communicate using essentially equal status with allowances for differences in power. Most of us don't want to be talked down to by a superior or to have subordinates fawning before us. We could avoid a lot of conflict in our professional and social lives if we could respond to each other as *people* and not positions or manifestations of power structures. Increasing our awareness of the ways we convey status and how they might be perceived is very important.

Status expressions are often subtle and embedded within cultures. A Russian student told me of his experience in the army watching veteran soldiers make small status challenges to officers fresh out of college by not buttoning the top button on their uniform jackets as per regulation. By ignoring that detail the officer accedes to the status challenge. A pilot friend talks about "right-seat captains," first officers who make potentially dangerous status challenges to the captain, who must maintain complete power and status for safety reasons.

Another student, who worked with Patch Adams, believes Adams has done so much good for patients because he assumes low status in their interactions, something traditionally rare between a doctor and patient, and thus is able to respond to and affect them in ways he couldn't otherwise. The famous quotation, "No man stands so tall as when he stoops to help a child," which has been attributed to many, suggests so much about the complex nature of status.

Regardless of whether or not you agree with my assertions about status, I encourage you to reflect on your own status behaviors, animal, civil, or whatever you want to call them. Observe status displays in other people and animals. You can do it in person, on screen, or onstage. What seems to work best for you and others?

You might discover you have a default animal-status setting, which is how you perceive your power or even competence relative to others. That setting is likely to vary according to the situation. Does your default status serve you well?

Low default animal status is the most common and limiting status problem I see in my work. If you present your ideas from too-low status, you're undercutting them. Some people can't even pretend to have high status, no matter how much coaching they get. Some people confuse high animal status with low civil status. The ability to be big and loud doesn't make you bad, it just makes you more expressive. Being bad makes you bad.

Some of us are addicted to apologizing. We apologize for everything, including things that aren't our fault, things that don't warrant an apology, and even, when confronted with them, our apologies themselves. This constant apologizing not only fritters away our status but also devalues the act of apologizing. A sincere apology is a beautiful thing, one that combines the highest civil status with low animal status. We could use more sincere apologies in the world. We could also do without knee-jerk apologies that mean and do nothing.

"No one can make you feel inferior without your permission," Eleanor Roosevelt once said, and I believe her statement relates directly to status. We've all got to stand up for ourselves! If we aren't capable of using high-status behavior at times, we might not be able to get our messages across effectively.

In a public-speaking class I had a student who was quite dynamic and possessed an engaging communication style. But when she practiced her speech, her manner became very flat. When I mentioned this, she said she was toning down her presentation because it was for university department heads and surgeons. "Do you want to bore them?" I asked. She replied no but that she wanted to show respect for their authority. I said I doubted her audience, regardless of its power and expertise, wanted to see her as a drone or peon. If she was taking their time, she should do so respectfully but confidently.

Healthy people in positions of power don't need to be constantly reminded of their authority. They want you to get on with what you have to say. It's sort of like God in *Monty Python and the Holy Grail*, who grouses when he appears to King Arthur, "Oh, stop averting your eyes.... It's always, 'Oh I'm not worthy this' and 'Forgive me that...'"[42] I can't say for certain that this applies to deities, but I think it applies to most people in positions of authority. That said, some deference is appropriate. We should avoid displaying status too high for our power and position and appearing as a disrespectful hotshot who's a threat to authority.

High default animal status is much rarer than low default status, at least among people with whom I've worked over the years. A default status that's too high can make one come off as arrogant, cocky, insensitive, and indifferent. This can be true for people who have spotless ethics and the best intentions in the world.

I always assume people are trying to live with high civil status, being good people doing the right thing and doing it well. That endeavor involves the balancing act of animal behavioral status. Awareness and practice help us get better at it.

Exercises

Individual

1. Watch a movie or TV scene, and identify the status behaviors, challenges, tactics and shifts.
2. As if posing for a photograph, practice high animal-status positions and then practice low. You can mimic animals or just use human poses. Pay attention to your entire body, including your posture, legs, arms, and even fingers. Notice the way you look at things depending upon the status you're trying to project. If you feel so inclined, take some photos of your poses in a full-length mirror.
3. Practice high and low vocal styles with your voice. Try impressions of authority figures like politicians, announcers, and so on. Play with low-status affectations. Imagine yourself powerless. Note not just your tone and volume but also your pacing. If you end a sentence with an up note, as one would with a question, how does that affect the status?

Group

1. **Boss/Smith**

   You can find the original Sir/Smith in Keith Johnstone's *Impro* (cited above). Below is my adaptation of Johnstone's script. You can also write your own script. No matter which script you use, I suggest you laminate it, as the scene can get intense and mere paper often can't stand up to that. Don't make your players memorize the script. You can definitely do this exercise successfully online, although its potential is more limited than in person. Share your script in advance or through your app's chat feature.

Boss/Smith

Smith knocks on Boss' office door.
Boss: Come in.
Smith: You wanted to see me, Boss?
Boss: Yes. Please sit down, Smith. I suppose you know why I sent for you.
Smith: No, Boss.
Boss shows document to Smith. Smith reads it.
Smith: Ah yes, I can explain this fully.
Boss: You know this is cause for dismissal, don't you?
Smith: Won't you reconsider?

Boss: Goodbye, Smith.
SMITH: I never wanted this job anyway.
Exit Smith.

>   Try some variations.
>
>   A. Reverse Status: player with high power has low animal status and vice versa.
>   B. Switch: One player has high status and the other low, and then they swap status at the director's signal.
>   C. Status Tower: Each line must be read with animal status that tops the previous line.
>   D. Status Tunnel: Same as the Tower only you're using progressively lower status.
>   E. High Animal Meets High Civil.
>   F. Come up with your own (and share them with me).

2. **Power-Pose-Off**

Participants or maybe just a few volunteers explore ways of posing powerfully. Try standing, sitting, and perhaps other positions. I haven't tried this game online, but it would be interesting to try. Players' relationship to the camera lens and how much space they take up in the frame would affect this as much as the poses themselves.

16

The Reason of Emotion and the Strength of Vulnerability

"It's not enough for a man to be known. A man must be felt."—Robert Frost

Emotion is the most important thematic ingredient in improv. You're welcome to disagree, but emotion is certainly the realm I explore more than any other as a director, teacher, and actor. Emotion drives characters and thus scenes. Improv without emotion lacks intensity, soul, and warmth.

Emotionless improv also lacks stakes. If the characters aren't facing risks and consequences, then the scene lacks importance and drive. Characters must be vulnerable to other characters and to circumstances for the audience to identify with and care about them.

It's fairly easy to understand the importance of emotion and vulnerability onstage and screen, in improvised and scripted forms. Yet we as a society tend to misunderstand and thus discount emotion and vulnerability in professional situations. This isn't surprising considering we're largely taught that being emotional in business is a sign of weakness and indicates that one can't be trusted or taken seriously. Certainly we want to avoid being inappropriate in the professional sphere, yet I feel we tend to throw the baby out with the bathwater when it comes to emotion and vulnerability in the real world.

Sometimes I like to ask my classes if emotions have a place in business. Some students say yes, and some say no. The question is ultimately pointless because, whether or not they belong, emotions *are* in business. All sorts of emotions are. I think most of us know that, but we get stuck on the question of whether or not emotions *should* be there.

Think for a moment about how we react in emotionally positive ways to others in professional situations. Based on my experience and talking with others, we want to do business with people who are not only competent but also trustworthy and likable. If these people are empathetic, inspiring, interesting, and funny, that's a bonus. These are some of the qualities we think of when we talk about emotional intelligence.

But don't just take my word for it. In 1999 Dr. Cary Cherniss assembled an impressive and lengthy list of examples that "build a case for how emotional intelligence contributes to the bottom line in any work organization."[43] Cherniss is the director and co-chair (with Daniel Goleman) of the Consortium for Research on Emotional Intelligence in Organizations and is also Director of the Organizational Psychology program at Rutgers University.

Let me emphasize that competence is crucial and that it's not enough just to be "nice." If you're a lousy businessperson, doctor, or lawyer but a good and accessible person, that doesn't change the fact that you'll probably have trouble succeeding in your profession unless you develop your occupation-specific skills. By the same token, highly proficient professionals can run into serious career trouble by being unable to connect on a personal level with their clients and colleagues.

It's worth noting that different cultures around the world devote varying amounts of time to establishing personal connections before, during, and after business interactions. If you're in Turkey, for instance, it would behoove you to understand that you'll make small talk over tea before talking turkey. Americans, by contrast, are notoriously quick to get past the niceties and down to brass tacks.[44]

Job interviews are largely about exploring personal connections and soft skills. Potential employers have had a chance to see candidates' résumés and have a sense of their qualifications. In interviews employers want to make sure new hires fit in their cultures and, presumably, that they're pleasant and even fun to work with. Potential employees (should) consider these same things during these interactions.

Conveying information is essential for people presenting in professional situations, be their audience one or one thousand. I wouldn't be as quick to say that emotion is the most important theme in business communication as it is in improv. Still, emotion makes a message more understandable—and thus stronger—by suggesting not only how the audience might think but also how it might feel about the message. Emotion adds the "why" to the "what," the meaning to the data, and taps into the audience's self-interest in the manner we explored in the Rip Van Winkle game.

What I'm getting at here is that your likeability, your *humanity* could be a competitive advantage in addition to being just a nice thing. Emotionally intelligent people are comfortable with feelings and know how to make use of them, ideally in enlightened, ethical, and nonexploitative ways.

Yet expressing emotion can be difficult for a number of reasons, and three I'd like to explore here are:

- Vulnerability
- Perspective
- Culture

Vulnerability

Being expressive makes us feel vulnerable, which is a difficult sensation to experience. For starters we have strong instinctual predispositions to avoid vulnerability because we seek security from danger, which fear can indicate. Atop this instinctual base we receive teaching and socializing to avoid being vulnerable, again because it's a threat to security. On a personal level, when we're vulnerable we risk misunderstanding and rejection, which cause emotional pain.

Yet there's a very strong relationship between vulnerability and trust, a phenomenon that is both intellectual and emotional. Trust might be the most important component of business relations, and no less a mainstream source than Forbes has asserted, "Trust is the new core of leadership."[45]

I'd even go so far as to say that you can't trust someone who's invulnerable. Trust depends upon mutual risk exposure, and if one is invulnerable, there can be no risk. Again, don't just take my word for it. In their 2015 paper, "Vulnerability and Trust in Leader-Follower Relationships," the authors conclude that there is a "need to risk willingness to be vulnerable as a base for trusting behavior. There is no way around being willing to be vulnerable."[46]

So imagine someone is taking a photo of you, and the caption will read "Trust me." What does that look like? Your body will probably be open with your arms partially extended and palms up to show that you're not a threat and that you're willing to trust the other party. In other words, you're physically vulnerable. And if the caption is "Don't trust me," you're probably closing yourself off for protection and your hands are out of sight, perhaps to hide weapons.

While we often fail to recognize vulnerability as a necessary element of trust, we also tend to conflate it with weakness. It's kind of like confusing envy with jealousy. Envy is desiring something someone else has, while jealousy is insecurity and fear of loss. The emotions have a similar sensation and some commonalities but are not the same thing. Likewise, vulnerability might mean unguardedness and a subsequent openness to harm, but it can also indicate a strength that requires no guardedness, a confidence in one's ability to handle a situation.

As counterintuitive as it seems, I believe that vulnerability is a sign of strength. It takes courage and boldness to present oneself openly. Acknowledging one's flaws and emotions—again, one's humanity—takes guts and is a sign of integrity.

Audiences tend to respond positively to vulnerability because it not only allows them to trust the speaker, but it also allows them to identify with the speaker, just as audiences identify with characters onstage or screen. When speakers share themselves, you feel connected to and familiar with them. Your mirror neurons provide the neurophysiological underpinning for what's also common psychological and sociological sense.

Catharsis, which I mentioned in an earlier chapter, is the releasing of strong or repressed emotions and relates to the effect described above. Cathartic outlets can take many forms: the arts, spectator sports, religion, nature, amusement park rides, and so on. I imagine it's a rare person who doesn't crave some form of catharsis.

Catharsis can also occur as we interact with people around us, although it's usually not as intense as, say, *Oedipus Rex* or a rollercoaster. We crave inspiration and reassurance from leaders. We want to feel bonds of loyalty and affection, the experience of belonging in a group. So when we provide the emotional handholds for people to connect with us, we're giving them what they want. Unless we open ourselves and trust that vulnerability isn't the same thing as weakness, any more than fear is danger, we can't connect with other people.

Now some of you might read that and think I'm advocating emotional incontinence, a lack of self-control, and chaos. I'm not. That would be the extreme end of the spectrum. What I am suggesting is that we go part of the way along the spectrum and discover what works. Going part of the way is not going all the way.

Perspective

We feel our emotions strongly, even though we often repress them, because we're close to them. We are, after all, the ones experiencing them. Our very proximity to our emotions can deceive us into thinking others sense them as strongly and clearly as we do. This might be a corollary to the spotlight effect, which puts us in the center of everyone else's world in addition to our own.

Furthermore, as I stated above, most of us are taught and socialized to avoid being inappropriately expressive. Of the people I've encountered in my work as a teacher and consultant, virtually none has been emotionally volatile and out of control, at least not in professional situations. Yet I have worked with many, many people who are inexpressive and lack dynamism. In other words, they're boring— at least on the outside. On the inside it's usually a different story, and so the challenge is to bring what's on the inside to the outside.

It's essential for actors and nonactors alike to remember that audiences can't see feelings. As discussed in an earlier chapter, audiences can only see behavior and infer from that what the presenter's emotional state is. That can be a good thing, and it can be a bad thing. If you're trying to appear cool when you're anxious, behave as if you feel cool and hope for the best. If you want to communicate enthusiasm, you'll similarly need to embody that and give it voice. Your audience isn't going to read your mind, but they will read your body.

Some people claim that they're an open book emotionally, that they have the opposite of a poker face. I suspect that these people are basing this assumption on a very small statistical sample of feedback from others who might well be close friends or family. I think most of us are better at hiding our emotions and worse at expressing them than we think we are. There are certainly times when it's appropriate for us to hide our true feelings, just as there are times when it's appropriate for us to display them. Either way, we need to employ good technique to convey our emotional message.

This technique, in a word, is exaggeration and that tends to feel fake or corny. Getting past that is crucial to developing one's expressiveness. Think about it; exaggerating empathy or enthusiasm can seem artificial, but, really, how is it different from raising your voice, using illustrative gestures, or speaking more clearly if someone can't understand you?

Exaggeration might feel overdone on the inside, but, as mentioned in the FIZ chapter, on the outside it might come off as just right. Time and again I see this in classes and workshops. The speaker or actor feels they're overacting to a terrible extent, but the audience feels the emotional tone is clear and appropriate. When I did studio voice work I almost always had to push my emotional message to a degree that felt artificial and overdone in order for it to satisfy the client and production team.

Ultimately I feel one must master exaggeration before one can master subtlety. The expert actor or presenter must know the potential of the many ways to convey an idea or feeling. And how will you know how effective and dynamic a communicator you can be unless you explore extremes? Maybe you're better than you think you are. Maybe by going too far you'll find power and depth in your message that remain even when you've reeled it back to a subtler level. You might not have found that power and depth had you not dared to stretch what you thought were your limits.

Just like everyone else, I find myself occasionally not feeling the way I wish I did at work and elsewhere. Maybe I'm tired, depressed, or annoyed while teaching or consulting. Perhaps I'm dissatisfied with the size or responsiveness of an audience for a show or even disappointed with the show itself. While it's important to acknowledge these feelings, it's also important to understand that if I make them too obvious, there could be negative effects on the proceedings; my class might lose energy, my client might feel offended, or my audience might feel unappreciated and disappointed.

So I need to behave in the way I *wish* I felt and trust that good things will come from that. If I can force some enthusiasm, my students might catch it, and I'll get caught up in that momentum. If I can patiently indulge that garrulous program participant, maybe they'll feel heard and feel more inclined to listen to others. Most show audiences have no idea whether or not they or the performance is living up to the performer's expectations as long as the performer stays upbeat. I have to work harder on some days than on others to create the best emotional atmosphere for my work.

Culture

Two of the biggest obstacles to expressiveness in contemporary American society (and likely elsewhere) are cynicism and irony. There was once a time in this country when openly sharing many emotions, particularly positive ones, was a standard thing. The evidence I offer comes from old films, TV, radio, and other media. People are often so jolly and enthusiastic in these relics that they seem downright goofy or even cloying from a modern perspective.

Even before the advent of electronic media, Americans were considered more open and less sophisticated than their European counterparts. The differences between New World and Old World behavior and society were documented by American authors such as Henry James and Mark Twain and European writers including Alexis de Tocqueville and Francois-René de Chateaubriand.

So what happened? In a nutshell I'd say, "The 1960s." It's more complicated than that though. Perhaps "postmodernism" is a more apt term. In World War II's wake, many people rethought a lot of the positive assumptions they had about humanity, society, and progress. It was hard to be naïve and optimistic after all that terror and destruction.

From a cinematic perspective, you can see this transformation very clearly in Westerns. Gary Cooper in *High Noon* (1952) is a flawed character, struggling with circumstances and an awareness of his own shortcomings. He is, perhaps, the first great antihero in film, in this case a man who performs heroic acts while lacking a classically heroic personality. Contrast this with John Wayne in *Stagecoach* (1939), who plays a man who seems the very embodiment of strength and competence and is untroubled by self-doubt, a traditional hero. I find *High Noon* to be a much more compelling film because of the lead character's vulnerability, so at this point postmodernism is a good thing.

As time passes in American film, we see the rise and evolution of the antihero. This character is not only flawed but comes to be increasingly at odds with society. So by 1955 we have *Rebel Without a Cause* starring James Dean, the title of which hardly needs explaining. By the 1970s the antihero in American cinema had become the norm, with actors like Jack Nicholson and Dustin Hoffman playing extremely antiheroic characters in films like *Five Easy Pieces* and *Midnight Cowboy*. By now the antihero could often be a downright villain, almost completely devoid of both classically heroic traits and deeds.

As discussed in Chapter 13, acting styles also changed over the decades from the expressionism that is the hallmark of traditional theatrical acting and silent movies to the understated, more intimate Method that relies on the camera to reveal it. One might assert that film themes also became more realistic, but you'd also have to concede that all this realism had an effect on the society cinema was portraying. And I'm focusing on film acting here because that's where most nonactors in my programs get most of their exposure to acting styles.

In addition to film and other art forms, comedy in general has become increasingly ironic over the decades, although this hasn't always been a linear progression. Irony is akin to sarcasm in that we're asserting something that isn't necessarily true and/or that might be the opposite of what we intend or actually believe. Irony and sarcasm are commentary at arm's length.

Detachment from and rebellion against society reflected the mindset of much of the 1960s' counterculture movement, which was disaffected by what it perceived as the mainstream's repression and violence. As this movement and its members aged, rebellion itself became mainstream. The rebellion that was once the province of adolescence has now become a lifelong attitude.

And speaking of adolescence, one of its first manifestations is when young people stop displaying and professing affection for things they have liked so far, things like parents, toys, and entertainment. If you've spent time among kids ages 12–14 (or so), you might well think they don't like *anything*. The fact is that they're just letting go of the old and discovering the new and also doing their best to hide their vulnerability and insecurity in this strange new world they're entering. They're hedging their bets about the things they like, waiting to see how their counterparts reveal how they feel.

Given this cultural and developmental backdrop, it can hardly be surprising that ordinary people are hesitant to show that they're gung ho. What was once considered a sign of being a decent and upstanding person is now seen as being a Pollyanna and a conformist—although one must wonder to what, seeing as how nonconformity is the new conformity.

This can be sad. Too many times I've heard students preface something heartfelt and positive by saying, "This might sound cheesy." That's not only sad, but it's also very hard to translate for international students. Cheesy, corny, what do we have against these foods?

Indifference is a safe—and boring—position in improv and in real life. If you decide you'd like to be more expressive, to positively affect your own life and the lives of those around you, you'll have to get outside of your comfort zone. You might have to push a little to make what's obvious on the inside obvious to those on the outside.

And if you really don't care and don't have strong feelings to express, then I think that's very sad indeed. But all is not lost because I feel that you can successfully employ the old "fake it 'til you make it" approach. Act in the way you wish you felt. Think about it; there's scientific evidence that suggests we wind up feeling the way we behave. So maybe by pretending to care, you can actually become a more caring person.

Writer Jean Giraudoux said, "The secret of success is sincerity. Once you can fake that you've got it made." I'm going to interpret that as a hopeful message grounded in science rather than merely a cynical witticism.

Exercises

Individual

The nature of expression is such that it's extremely difficult to work on it individually. How well you're expressing yourself all but demands an external perspective, seeing as your internal perspective is subjective and inaccurate. So working solo requires some disembodiment or collaboration with a partner, whether that partner knows it or not.

1. Record yourself. Using audio and/or on video, speak about something. It could be a formal or informal speech you're working on, a monologue from a play, or a stand-up routine. You can also use the One-Minute Passionate Presentation

below. Use the coaching criteria listed for that exercise to give yourself feedback. See if you can keep increasing the expressiveness until it gets to the point that it's obviously ridiculous; the point of the exercise is to stretch yourself, not to produce a refined product.

2. Experiment with others. This is often best done with strangers because it affords you anonymity and thus fewer consequences as you try out new things. See if you can be the Friendliest Person on Earth to the barista or bus driver. Try being the World's Best Listener for someone else. Obviously, focusing on positive emotions is the best approach. You might even try this exercise when you're going to deal with someone in a potential conflict or impersonal situation. Maybe you're at the DMV or talking on the phone to someone in customer service. See if you can't make a connection. Brighten the other person's day. Make them love you. Experience tells me it's not only a pleasant way to self-improvement but also a great way to get others to help you.

Group

1. **Emotions Party** (I think this is too complicated to play online.)

   A. Ask for four volunteers, and have one of them host a party onstage.

   B. Give the players three ways of feeling about someone else. I like to go with one very positive, one very negative, and one fairly neutral emotion.

   C. Each of the four players *secretly* assigns each of the emotions to the other three players, meaning that's how that player's character feels about the other three characters. Example: The emotions are love, hate, and confusion. Person A decides to love B, hate C, and be confused by D. But A can decide to love D, hate B, and be confused by C. Any combination works. Meanwhile B, C, and D are assigning love, hate, and confusion as their filters toward the other players' characters. It might turn out that A loves B and B loves A. Or A might love B and B hates A. There are many possibilities.

   D. Make it clear to the players that the exercise depends

upon their remembering how their character feels about the other characters and not changing their emotions regardless of how they're treated.

 E. Emphasize that the exercise isn't about subtlety or social convention and that you might ask the players during the exercise to make it clearer how their character feels about another.

 F. Start the scene with the host getting ready for the party.

 G. Guests enter one at a time when you make a ding-dong or knock-knock sound. They interact with the host and other guests based on the emotions they have assigned to those characters. Chaos will likely ensue.

 H. End the scene once everyone is involved and it seems to have run its course.

 I. Ask the audience what worked. Ask the players how it went for them. You might hear that what the players thought they were exaggerating wasn't that obvious to the other players or audience.

 J. Play the game a couple times with different players and different emotions. (I never tire of this game.)

2. **Emotional Rollercoaster (EmoRoCo)**

 A classic improv game, EmoRoCo requires two players and a director. It can be played online.

 A. Ask for two volunteers.

 B. Explain that the volunteers will start a scene and that you, the director, will call the name of one of the players and then state an emotion or state of consciousness. For example, "Cameron, sad." Cameron then plays sad as strongly as she can, without explaining why she is sad, until the director gives her a new emotion, at which point she drops sad completely and focuses on the new suggestion. Meanwhile the director is also giving suggestions to the other player in the same manner. The emotions can be feelings or just an adjustment an actor can make, such as being French or a cat.

 C. Solicit a location from your audience, and have the two volunteers start a scene in that place.

 D. This exercise can be done silently, which can work for people who are just learning a language or for people who rely too heavily on talking.

E. End the exercise at a high point, and then ask the players how it went for them. Ask the audience about their response. You might find, again, that players think they're being overly obvious when they're actually being understated.

F. Play the game a few times. Invite your audience to suggest emotions and other adjustments. Maybe someone else would like to try directing. Coach the players to focus increasingly on *showing* the emotion through their behavior rather than *telling* it by announcing it.

3. **One-Minute Passionate Presentation** (works online)

A. Ask for a volunteer to make a one-minute speech.

B. The topic can be anything, but the speaker's goal is to convey their strong emotions about it. The subject can be something big, like social justice, or something seemingly insignificant, like cookies. My only off-limit topic is being a fan of a sports team (even though I'm a sports fan) because it's too safe and it's more cathartic than direct experience.

C. Emphasize that the speech will be evaluated based on emotion conveyed, not content. To that end, speakers may speak in their first language because the audience can still understand the feelings even if it can't understand the words. Listening to a short speech in a language you don't understand can be exciting, and not only will you be fortunate to hear it, but you'll also afford a non-native speaker to present with the linguistic confidence the rest of us take for granted.

D. Take notes on what the speaker does to enhance their expressiveness and what they do that detracts from it. Be on the lookout for meaningless gestures that fritter away energy.

E. When a speaker finishes, ask the audience what emotions they sensed. If the discussion starts focusing on content, direct it back toward expressiveness.

F. Share your own feedback and coach the speakers.

G. If you feel it's beneficial, have speakers do part of the speech again, focusing on being deliberate. Get them to go big! You can also have speakers repeat parts of the speech with the filter that the audience is something different, like a bunch of little kids, friends at a bar, grandparents, a Nobel Prize committee, etc.

H. The exercise is about reaching the hearts of your audience. A clear, powerful emotional message can complement your rational message.

4. **Interpretation**

   I learned this game as a gibberish exercise, but it went from being challenging fun to profound when I started working with international students. One suggested we had enough linguistic diversity to play with actual languages rather than gibberish. So try that if you can. Interpretation can be played online.

   I. Ask for three volunteers. Two will engage in a discussion. The third will be the interpreter, translating into English (or whatever language is predominant in your group) what the other two are saying to each other.

   J. If you're using gibberish, anyone can play any role. If you're using actual languages, the parties discussing a topic should not speak each other's language, and the interpreter should speak neither language. For example, Party A might speak Hindi, and Party B might speak Dutch. If so, Party A shouldn't understand Dutch, Party B shouldn't understand Hindi, and the interpreter shouldn't understand Hindi or Dutch.

   K. Give the two parties something to discuss. It could be anything from resolving an intergalactic crisis to visiting a therapist. Direct them to speak short, clear sentences and to use clear body language while avoiding outright signing.

   L. Instruct the interpreter to mirror the parties' gestures— the body might understand what the message is before the mind does—and to use first-person pronouns instead of third-person. Emphasize to the interpreter that they're only offering an impression of what's being said, not a word-for-word translation. The interpreter must become transparent, seeking only to serve the other parties and not the self.

   M. Once the game starts, you might need to coach the players with reminders about these directions. You also might need to coach the parties through conflict or get them out of exchanges that have devolved into mere numeric bargaining. Definitely keep an eye out for an interpreter starting to make stuff up on their own rather than responding to the other parties.

N. End the exercise at a high point or a dead end. Ask the parties how much of their exchanges the interpreter expressed correctly. Discuss and repeat if you like. This is a risky exercise in that so much depends upon the interpreter. At worst it's amusing. At best it illustrates better than any other exercise that, where meaning is concerned, it's not what you say but how you say it.

17

Tabula Rasa

The Blank Slate

"You can observe a lot just by watching."—Yogi Berra

Sometime in the 1990s I came up with an idea for players *not* to have ideas. I'd noticed that the improvisers I was directing and I would occasionally miss what was actually happening in a scene because we were so busy trying to figure out what was happening or trying to make something happen. We seemed to lose awareness of our partners and start thinking more about ourselves and our own ideas.

What if players could have an empty mind and focus solely on reacting to their partners, I wondered. Could the jumble of thoughts be replaced by *nothing*? The term *tabula rasa* came to mind. It's Latin for "blank slate" (a slate being the handheld chalkboard or wax-covered tablet students used to use in schools), and educators have used the term to describe how students theoretically approach a subject, with no preexisting thoughts or prejudices.

Around this time I was exposed to the work of Sanford Meisner, an actor and acting teacher who emphasized responding to other actors as opposed to focusing so much on one's self and character.[47] Some Meisner work involves repetition, actors repeating (repeatedly) what the other has said. I liked how this approach made me aware of and connected to my fellow players. I wondered if there was a way to develop something similar for improvisers, actors who don't have a script or story to guide them.

Rather than have players repeat what the other has said, I decided to have players say aloud what the other was doing. I had two actors sit at a 90-degree angle to each other so that both they and the audience could see their behavior. Then they'd trade obser-vations about what each was doing (disregarding clothing, grooming, and physical attributes because in improv these are usually imagined and not based on reality). It would go something like this:

CAMERON: Jordan, your right leg is crossed over your left.
JORDAN: Cameron, your hands are clasped, and you're tapping your fore-finger on the knuckles of your opposite hand.
CAMERON: Jordan, you nodded as you made that observation.
JORDAN: Cameron, your voice rose as you said that.

Okay, it sounds like an encounter group from the '70s so far, and maybe it is. But the players are paying attention to *each other*. At times intense scrutiny is required because players can get pretty still, and they might wind up noticing their partner's breath or posture. They might feel self-conscious about their observations about their part-ner as well as their partner's observations about them. However, with practice they can focus more and more on the partner and less and less on the self. Their minds can become blank slates to be filled with responses to their partners, and thus I called this exercise Tabula Rasa.

After each player makes three to four observations about their partner's behavior, the next step in the exercise is to have the players *interpret* their observations about each other's behavior. The inter-pretations can be realistic and obvious or fanciful and surprising. The exercise starts to sound like this:

CAMERON: Jordan, you just scratched your chin. You're trying to look wise.
JORDAN: Cameron, you chuckled slightly. You're proud of your clever remark.
CAMERON: Jordan, you just pressed your palm down against your thigh. You're smashing a butterfly.
JORDAN: Cameron, you're now leaning forward because you want to see the butterfly's guts.

Again, this ain't quite Shakespeare, but then it's not supposed to be. The players are now not only paying attention and respond-ing to each other, but they're also building meaning and context from what's transpiring between them. They can sense this as can the audi-ence. They're also starting to develop chemistry, which might appear hostile or affectionate but at its heart is playful. Players should have a playful relationship.

I like to get multiple pairs up to play the game as we explore it. Maybe we begin with one pair that only makes observations, and then we stop and take a moment to discuss what happened. Then we get a second pair up to make observations and interpretations and then stop to compare and contrast the different versions of the exercise. While I like to keep the momentum going, I also like to be sure that all the participants see and understand what we're doing and have a chance to comment or ask questions.

A question I like to ask the audience is, "Was that interesting to watch?" I almost always hear that it is, which shouldn't surprise me but does because the exercise is so simple. Something beyond mere words happens in this game. Maybe we pick up tension or chemistry, and thus I like to follow up with the question, "What happened?" The audience might not agree about what happened, but they usually agree that something was indeed happening.

The final iteration of this exercise has the players continuing to exchange observations and interpretations about each other's behavior, only now I set their interaction in a situation or place. It might be a job interview, a couple waiting to see a marriage counselor, a parent-teacher conference, a meeting between a parent-in-law-to-be and their child-in-law-to-be, an aging quarterback and a young quarterback on the sidelines. Imagination is the only limitation here, but I like scenarios with high stakes.

Now the players start to react to each other not only as actors but also in their characters, which are evolving. I tell them they can keep strictly to the exercise or get away from it. However, the players should be aware that their scene has grown from the exercise and that they can (and should) return to the exercise if they start to become disconnected or feel lost in the scene. Sometimes I call for players to return to observations and interpretations in order to reground the scene. Indeed the Tabula Rasa observe-and-interpret technique might be used in just about any scene whether or not it began with the actual exercise. It's an improv "life preserver," like getting physical or mirroring, that you can use if your scene starts to founder.

I believe that Tabula Rasa is a powerful performance technique because the audience sees the pairing of an objective observation that they too have witnessed with a subjective interpretation. They follow along step-by-step and see the scene develop just as the players do. You might say Tabula Rasa is an organic process. I like organic improv, in which the scenes are as much about what's actually transpiring onstage as they are about context and story.

It's worth noting that others might well have invented or used this exercise before I did. However, I didn't learn it from anyone else. While I'm proud of devising in a vacuum a way to solve an improv problem, I don't claim to have invented this exercise any more than any other in this book.

The value of Tabula Rasa—awareness, connection, creating chemistry between players, and getting players out of their heads and into the scene—is pretty clear for improvisers onstage. Now let's look at how Tabula Rasa can be used in nontheatrical situations.

Tabula Rasa players are often surprised by the mirror aspect of the exercise. They might not realize that they're doing the things their partners mention or might be surprised by how their behavior is interpreted. Thus, the exercise fosters physical self-awareness. Even when the interpretations of behavior are outrageous, the exercise can be a great way of starting a group discussion about body language.

You see, as ridiculous as some of the Tabula Rasa interpretations might be, this process of observing and interpreting mimics what we do in real life. We notice and try to make sense of physical behavior all the time, consciously and subconsciously, to the extent that we call it body language. That's probably why the exercise and technique resonate and create intensity onstage.

What can we glean from body language? What are others' bodies saying to us? My opinion is that body language is expressive but not particularly articulate. It's like if you put a gag on someone, you might not be able to understand what they're saying, but you'll probably get a general idea about their emotional state. (I bet you thought the gags I mentioned in this book would be figurative, not literal.)

Crossed arms, for example, are generally interpreted to mean that one is closed off to others or perhaps to others' ideas. As a teacher I'm very sensitive to this in the classroom. Yet I see students with crossed arms who are clearly engaged. Their arms might be crossed because they're cold or because they're nursing an injury or because it's simply comfortable. Or maybe they *are* closed to me and my ideas. The whole picture, the context of the closed arms, is going to tell me a lot more than just the closed arms themselves.

Similarly, I once read that if a person touches their nose when they're speaking, that's an indication that they're lying. Well, I've been talking to someone and felt my nose itch and scratched it without fibbing. I've also been talking to someone when I've had nasal issues and made a quick check to make sure nothing gross was going on in the nostril area, a bat in the cave if you will, and again it hasn't turned me into a dishonest person. That said, maybe my counterpart in these conversations focused on the nose-touching and figured me for a big liar.

My point is that we must be very cautious interpreting others' body language because it can contain mixed signals. And that's not even touching on international differences in overt and subtle body language. Sure, there are experts at "reading" people, but these experts are detectives, behaviorists, poker players, and the like and have extensive experience and training. That's their thing. For the rest of us, reading people can be a matter of a little knowledge being a dangerous thing, and we run the very real risk of projecting our feelings, thoughts, and perceptions onto others rather than being aware of and open to them. Know the difference between objective observation and subjective interpretation; again, see what you see, not what you think you see.

So I say don't think you *know* how someone feels or what they think based on their body language. However, you should be sensitive to others' body language and respond accordingly. You might even ask, diplomatically, if your intuition based on body language is correct. Do you have a question? Have I said something offensive? Would you like to take a short break?

Now the unfair flip side of the body-language coin is that you can't expect others to be as thoughtful and equanimous with regard to your physical behavior. Instead you must be aware of the potential messages you're sending with your posture, gestures, facial expressions, and vocal tone and understand that others might draw conclusions from them.

If you want to convey that you're open to a person, make sure you're not crossing your arms. If you have something very important to tell someone, avoid touching your nose lest that person think you're lying because they read that nose-touching betrays dishonesty. I could go on with a list of dos and don't-dos, but I address physical self-awareness and control elsewhere in this book. I also try to avoid prescribing or proscribing specific behavior and prefer that people figure out on their own what works and what doesn't.

What else is useful about Tabula Rasa?

Well, there's the blankness of that blank slate. Like I said earlier, I devised this exercise because I wanted my players *not* to have ideas but to be open to whatever might arise in scenes with each other.

This might seem like a mixed message. After all, we've explored ways of generating ideas in this book, and now I'm saying not to have them. My actual goal is to encourage you to keep an open mind. Just because you have what seems like a great idea doesn't mean that it can't be improved, that everyone else feels or thinks the same way, or that you can stop using "Yes-And."

A nontheatrical example might look like this. You have a great idea for a project. You've got the knowledge, the experience, and the creative spark. However, the idea is fully formed in your head, and you're resistant to alterations or additions that others might have. This could result in a project that falls short of its potential because the vision is limited, and it could also cause interpersonal strife because you've rejected others' input.

Sometimes others' input *isn't* an improvement. If you can at least honestly entertain those suggestions, really be open to them and not just pay them lip service, the process will go better because the project will have been exposed to the acid test of possible improvement. That makes the concept stronger.

It's hard to expose your ideas, your darling ideas, to alteration by others though. Judging from my experience, most people new to improvising, onstage or off, are afraid they won't have ideas. Thus, they're overly protective of the ideas they do have because they feel there's a limited supply or even a desperate shortage of them. With practice most people get past that point and develop confidence in their creativity and its abundance.

When I first started in improv, I was confident in my ideation because I was an inveterate wiseass, a person who'd spent most of his school years, particularly grades six to 12, entertaining/annoying teachers and fellow students. I hadn't yet learned to trust the blank slate though. I was open to doing scenes based on my idea or someone else's idea, but I wasn't comfortable with the middle ground. So I suppose I was afraid of having my precious ideas changed because I worried I might not have more of them.

If you don't have a strong idea or an idea at all, the Tabula Rasa approach can help keep you calm. You can have faith in the process of knocking around concepts and creative impulses and then seeing them aggregate and mutate into useful fully formed plans. If you're relaxed and not panicked, your mind will be suppler and you'll be more creative. Creativity thrives best in relaxed, playful environments with relaxed, playful people.

Another way of exploring Tabula Rasa techniques is through interpretation or translation exercises. There are many of these in improv. One is the Interpretation game I described in the previous chapter. Another is known as Subtitles or Foreign Film, in which one or more players pretend to translate for other players doing a scene in gibberish or a foreign language. Play these games a few times, and you start to find "bits" or little recurring jokes, like a player saying something monosyllabic that the interpreter goes on at length about or vice versa.

I've even performed a game in which one player pretends to do sign language interpretation for two speakers in a talk-show format. In this case the spoken language is understood, while the translation is gibberish. I've seen audiences roar with laughter during performances of this game, and I'm not entirely sure why; I think there's something primal about it because it's so physical and absurd. Signers have told me that the gibberish is often close to actual sign language. I've had hearing-impaired audience members tell me that the humor comes not from making fun of sign language but from the futility of the impostor trying to sign.

Ultimately, Tabula Rasa not only means "blank slate" but also "empty mind." You might hear that term associated with meditation, and that seems appropriate. Meditation is a way to observe your thoughts without reacting toward them, to clear the clutter and quiet the noise inside.[48] By doing so you gain a sense of peace and focus that allows you to connect and respond better to the outside world. That's one of the goals of applied improv.

By employing Tabula Rasa techniques you are:

• Paying attention to others
• Being open to possibilities and opportunities
• Increasing the potential of collaboration
• Aware of but not mono-focused on yourself and
• Getting out of your head and into the moment.

Exercises

Individual

1. Do a Systems Check (described elsewhere in this book) based on your current physical position. Be aware of what you're

doing with your entire body, from your toes to the top of your head. Imagine what someone might infer from your posture, movement, and facial expression. Change one part of the picture, and see how it might change the overall effect. This is something you can practice when you're standing in a queue or riding a bus or train.

2. Try the observe-and-comment exercise, cautiously and diplomatically with someone else. Experiment playfully with a friend or family member in a low-pressure situation. Make sure they're open to it and not distracted. A perfect chance might be while you're waiting for food at a restaurant. A really bad place to try it for the first time would be during a job interview or couples counseling. Remember that projecting your emotions and thoughts onto someone else isn't healthy.

3. Once you've experimented with the exercise, you might employ it in more serious situations but always in a way that suggests a question and not a statement. For example, you might notice while you're interacting with a person that their arms are crossed and ask, "Are you comfortable with this conversation?" or "Would it be better to discuss this later?" The idea is that you're attentive and sensitive to your counterpart, not that you're judgmental or reading their mind. You don't want to put them on the spot. For example you probably wouldn't want to say, "Why are you blushing?"

Group

1. **Tabula Rasa**

   I've described the exercise above, so here I'll chart the progression. Trying to play this online raises the level of difficulty to the point that I'm not sure it would work.

   A. Two volunteers sit in front of the rest of the group and exchange observations about each other's behavior. Ignore clothing, grooming, and physical attributes. The players should try to behave as naturally as possible; this is not a contest to see who can be stillest or who can move the most.

   B. After three observations by each player, the director asks each player to pair a subjective interpretation, realistic or fanciful, with the objective observation.

Continue the exchanges for, say, five repetitions for each player.

   C. Ask the players how the exercise went for them. What did they think? How did they feel? Ask the audience about their response, and see where the discussion leads.

   D. Repeat steps A-C with two new players. Make a point to discuss the chemistry between the players. It tends to be either hostile or affectionate but rarely indifferent. What did the players feel? What did the audience observe?

   E. With two new players repeat steps A and B, and then have the director add a context to see what effect that has on the exchanges.

   F. If you're so inclined, especially if your group is focusing on stage performance, try step E and invite the players to let go of the rigid structure of the exercise and simply play the scene. But invite them to return to the structure temporarily if they feel they're losing connection to their partner or momentum in the scene. The director may also call for a return to observe-and-interpret exchanges.

2. **Foreign Film**

   A. Set up a scenario for two players. It can be based on a situation, place, relationship, or just about anything. The actors will speak to each other in gibberish and/or a foreign language.

   B. You can have a third player interpreting for both of the actors, or you can assign an interpreter for each actor.

   C. You can stage the interpreter(s) wherever you like: beside the actors, in the wings, downstage. Some people like to play it where the interpreters run in a crouch in front of the scene as though they were subtitles (yes, a person imitating imitation translation).

18

It's Not All About You and It's Not All Bad

How can we be sensitive to our audiences without being over-sensitive or getting the wrong idea about them? This is a complex question for which there's no definite answer. There are so many personal, cultural, and situational variables. Still, like most questions with uncertain answers, it's worth exploring. No doubt we want to be aware of and respond to our audience, whether it's one person or thousands.

I'd like to start by addressing the neurotic tendency we have to make ourselves the centers of an audience's universe just as we are the centers of our own. It's sort of like the spotlight effect, the illusion that we're the focus of attention, except that as a presenter or performer you probably *are* the focus of attention. What I'm talking about is an extension of that effect, thinking we're the cause of the audience's behavior. In other words, if someone or a group is behaving a certain way, it *must* be because of something we're doing. And it's probably bad.

As a performer and teacher I have decades of experience in front of audiences. I believe reading an audience is similar to reading body language in that both are intuitive and inexact skills that can often be inaccurate. Audiences are generally as inarticulate as body language is, and while one can usually infer an audience's general mood, anything beyond that is a real stretch.

If you've been in front of a lively audience, one that's with you all the way and hanging on every word, gesture, or note, you know what a wonderful, even transcendental, experience that is. I can even recall a few performances with houses so responsive that they felt artificial, like a very loud laugh track was playing. Such audiences can spoil you though and make you have unrealistic expectations.

I've often been spooked by what I felt were unenthusiastic and unresponsive audiences. "This audience is too quiet." "These people have no energy." These are things I'm prone to think and that I've heard others say when in front of an audience that isn't amazingly wonderful. And from those thoughts it's a short commute to, "They don't like me," and, "We're not doing well."

It's all about us and it's all bad.

Yet I recall doing improv shows for audiences I inferred didn't like the performance. Afterward I've talked to audience members and heard more than one person say things like, "We were afraid to laugh because we might miss a word." Admittedly, that's not a scientific survey, but I've performed long enough to know that if people think your show stinks, they won't hang around to talk to you afterward or they'll say something like, "Gee, it sure looked like you were having fun up there."

Maybe the audience is rapt, but the room is too hot; a cool room makes for a more alert and responsive audience. I've had fellow performers and directors aver that Friday audiences are less energetic than Saturday audiences because many of them are tired from the work week. And Sunday matinees? They're dead; any performer will tell you that. Why? Well, it's the middle of the calmest day of the week, and audiences tend to be smaller and older and so on and so on.

There was a casting director I used to read for regularly when auditioning for film and TV projects. Often she would be reading the character opposite mine in a two-person scene. I had difficulty playing scenes with her because she'd usually do them without emotion or energy. If your scene partner seems to be giving 15 percent, it's hard for you to give 100, particularly if the scene has high stakes.

The assumption I made was that she didn't like me as an actor or even as a person. But then I asked around to other actors and found they all received basically the same treatment. Then one day she cast me in a production! So she didn't hate me. But her way of reading with me never changed, and I eventually learned just to show up and deliver the best performance I could—and when should that not be the case? The casting director's approach might well have been genius. Or maybe it was the opposite. Either way, it had nothing to do with me.

As a teacher I've had class sessions that felt like a New Year's Eve party, and I've had other times when I felt I was losing the room or a student, based on subjective observations and intuition. Students might be yawning or looking out a window. That means I'm boring and the lesson plan sucks, right? Well, that *could* be the case. Or it could be that the yawning student was up all night drinking or even studying. And oftentimes when people are considering an idea, they'll look away, trying the idea on for size. The audience's response here might have nothing to do with me or it might be positive instead of negative or it could be a combination of all these things.

During the COVID pandemic, I struggled with class response because online teaching is so different from teaching in person, especially with interactive courses like mine. I could see when students were paying more attention to their phones than to me or their classmates. Aside from reminding them that the quality of the course depended largely on their engagement, there wasn't much I could do about it. Certainly the students suffered from Zoom fatigue and other pandemic stressors just as I had, and being a martinet about it would only make things worse. Some days I was so demoralized and exhausted, I could barely make it from the desk to the futon in my office for a nap after class.

Yet at the end of semesters, my students wanted to get their classes together in person just for fun. So many of them told me that my course was their favorite and sometimes the only one they felt compelled to attend and participate in during the pandemic. I was so surprised and, of course, delighted. You see, I'd been blinded by my own expectations. The students didn't have the in-person class with which to compare the online version. It was so challenging and even traumatic at times for me that I had to remind myself constantly that this could be the best (and, in fairness, usually the only) improv course my students had ever had. They literally didn't know what they were missing even if *I* had a hard time forgetting what they were missing. I had to get past that to succeed.

This can apply to so many experiences. Maybe you have a

standard presentation, pitch, monologue, or song you do. Sometimes it'll feel good and sometimes it'll feel bad, but you have to be open to the idea that the audience can love it even if you don't. Audiences go crazy when musicians perform their biggest hits in concert, even if it's the zillionth time for the musicians. Okay, maybe it only feels like the zillionth time, but the musicians have to think about the gift they're giving the audience, not just about themselves, and maybe someone's never heard the song before and can fall in love with it for the first time. Put another way, one of my students was a cross-country runner and told me the team's coach said, "just because you don't feel like you're running fast doesn't mean you're not."

Unfamiliar cultures can throw us too. A colleague told me a story about an American woman who was invited to make a presentation in South Korea. She'd never made a presentation outside of the USA, and, when she completed the first part and the group took a break, because she was distraught that the audience was so quiet, unexpressive, and unresponsive. She sought out her host, intending to offer to cancel the second part of her presentation because it was going so poorly. Before the speaker could make the offer, though, the smiling host said, "They love you!" The speaker was surprised by and not prepared for the audience response because she was used to the less reserved reception of American audiences. Of course, American audiences can vary greatly, as can audiences of all nationalities, be they in workplaces, concert halls, places of worship, schools, bars, or sports arenas.

Regardless of the setting or circumstances, whatever you're not used to can seem confusing, weird, and even frightening. People and situations are different, and their audience reactions might have little or nothing to do with you. And even if they do, you've still got a job to do, and you need to concentrate your energy on your performance rather than fretting about its reception.

Mockery of a Mock Interview is an exercise I developed for my business school classes. Job interviews are a concern for everyone at some point, and this low-stakes exercise gives people a chance to practice interviewing, to have a little fun with it, or to have the shoe on the other foot and be the interviewer rather than the interviewee. The setup is pretty simple, and it has a lot in common with several other improv games.

We start with two volunteers, one playing the interviewer and one the interviewee. I ask the interviewee to name a position for which they're qualified and that they'd also be excited to interview for. So if this person is studying marketing, perhaps there's a plum job with an outstanding firm that they'd be delighted to land. Interviewing to become CEO of a Fortune 500 company or the head coach of a professional sports team aren't such good choices here because they're not realistic enough for someone just out of an undergrad or graduate program, even though they might be exciting. The outlandish nature of such a scenario makes the stakes too low.

I emphasize to the interviewee that they should do their best to try to get the job. Take the interview seriously, and be yourself as much as you can. The exercise won't work if the interviewee plays it for laughs. Once I've given that direction, I send the interviewee out of the room with an escort to keep them company (and to keep them from eavesdropping).

Then I ask the rest of the class to think of distracting and/or disturbing behaviors we can give to the interviewer. Considering some of the interviewing horror stories I've heard, I think I could get ten such behaviors from every single person in the room! Pick the first three that seem suitable, meaning that they should be easy to do and be varied. For example, we might use something gestural, something vocal, and something having to do with eye contact. Also make sure the behaviors aren't too offensive or distasteful; when in doubt, simply ask the interviewer if they're comfortable doing the behavior in question.

Incidentally, I occasionally surprise the interviewee by having them return to the room to face two interviewers. This not only changes the power dynamic but also creates the opportunity for some of the distracting and/or disturbing behavior to involve the relationship between the two interviewers.

My direction to interviewers is to use the specific behaviors frequently and at different levels of intensity. I tell them that if they hear me snapping my fingers during the interview that means they need to use the behaviors more.

We call the interviewee back into the room, and the interview begins. The proceedings are usually pretty hilarious. From an improv standpoint, we have a scene between a dysfunctional or "crazy" character and a "straight man" (a generic term in comedy applied regardless of actual gender, identity, or sexual orientation). This is a very old and common trope in comedy. I believe it works because the audience identifies with the straight man, the Everyman, and has experienced times when they were the sane person trying to make sense of an insane situation.

Incidentally, experienced improvisers and actors know that being the straight man is often more difficult than being the dysfunctional character. The straight man has to remain understated and keep feeding the beast that is the dysfunctional character and its behavior. Straight man is an underappreciated supporting role that doesn't usually get the big accolades, sort of like a point guard dishing assists to scorers in basketball or a jazz pianist comping behind another player's solo.

The Mockery of a Mock Interview probably runs five minutes, although I confess I've never timed it. I end it when the players have had plenty of opportunity to play the scene and seem to be running out of energy or discoveries. Ending at a high point, like a hearty laugh or some resolution, is a bonus.

Once we're done, my first question is for the interviewee. I explain that we gave the interviewer three behaviors and ask if the interviewee can identify them. Sometimes they can. Nose-picking, for example, is hard to miss. But with other behaviors, the interviewee will often extrapolate to a conclusion beyond mere behavior. For example, we might have instructed the interviewer to avoid eye contact and to yawn. Most times the interviewee will see that and jump to the conclusion that the interviewer is uninterested in or even hostile to them. This makes sense, but what's striking is the way we piece together clues and reach conclusions about others' feelings about us, even in a simulated situation like this. Natural though it might be, we overlook the possibility that people we deal with are struggling with an issue utterly unrelated to us, perhaps a colicky baby, an ill parent, job worries, or just a plain old bad mood.

After hearing the interviewee discuss the interviewer's behavior, I ask both players how the exercise went for them. Often the interviewer will report they constantly and obviously did the behaviors suggested by the audience. But often that's not the case objectively. This jibes with my assertion that what's clear on the inside is not always or even usually clear on the outside.

The interviewee will generally feel a little like they've been ambushed, and that's entirely understandable. The exercise is challenging, and the interviewee is trying to be successful and collected in a situation that's unexpectedly crazy. In addition the interviewee likely wants to show off their interviewing skill for the audience and be judged favorably. The setup, interviewing for a job they'd like, is realistic even if the actual interview isn't, so this can hit a little close to home. Usually the interviewee's opinion of their performance is low and lower than the audience's or mine. I make a point to ask the audience what they observed and how they thought the players did, and I'll add my own comments.

This exercise tends to be a win-win for the players. If the interview is a disaster, it becomes comedy and provokes a lot of laughter. Both players can take pride in the humorous scene they've created even—especially—if the interview itself was a failure. If the interviewee handles the absurd situation really well, it might not have been as amusing an improv scene as the disastrous encounter, but the interviewee will have earned kudos for their composure. I mention this because I want the interviewee to feel good about their performance; if they do, then they and others will be more open to learning from the exercise.

The players can teach us much by example. Some interviewees won't react to the interviewer's strange behavior or adapt their presentation style to the situation. Many times I've seen interviewees drone on and on even though the interviewer seems distracted. More skillful interviewees alter their tone, their posture, or their energy in order to engage with the interviewer. The interviewee might even politely suggest that the interviewer seems distracted and that there might be a better time for the interview. In other words, they respond to the reality of the situation rather than sticking doggedly to a plan that appears not to be working. Naturally, this can be taken too far; you wouldn't want to insult or get presumptuous with an interviewer. A gentle "I-statement" couched in subjectivity, as opposed to a pointed "you statement" that assumes objectivity, can be both appropriate and effective.[49]

Another thing to remember about being in front of an audience, especially in interview situations, is that the interviewee has a right to dignity and decent treatment. A job interview is, theoretically at least, a two-way interaction and both parties are trying to sell the other on what they have to offer. Both parties should be respectful and even friendly. Many interviewers will try to challenge interviewees, and that's part of the game. If the challenge turns to abasement or abuse, the interviewee would do well to remember their self-respect and consider whether or not they want to deal with such treatment every working day.

So to sum it up when you're in front of an audience:

- Be aware of your audience, one or many people, but don't presume to read their minds.
- Cultural, environmental, or other factors might make it appear that your audience isn't engaged or enthusiastic when it actually is.
- Don't assume that you're the center of everyone else's world, that you're the cause of their behavior, and that their responses to you are negative.
- That said, if your audience seems disengaged or bored, they might be, so you might enliven or alter your delivery.
- Remember why you're there, and focus on presenting what you came to present, adapting as necessary. For example, if someone has a question, answer *that* question rather than trying to force a preplanned response. Allow some leeway in discussion; you might wind up exploring something even better and more relevant than what you had planned.
- Where time is concerned, it's almost always better to go short than long. It's like the old showbiz saw, "Always leave 'em wanting more." Think about it; when was the last time you were disappointed a presentation or meeting ended early? Focus on impact rather than duration.
- Don't tolerate blatantly disrespectful or abusive behavior.

Exercises

Individual

1. **Reflection**
   Think back on your experiences as a presenter, either in one-on-one or group settings:
   A. How did you feel about your experience?
   B. Do you *know* how the audience received you? How do you know?
   C. Have you made assumptions about the way your audience received you, either at the time or afterward?
   D. What would you do differently?

2. Try the individual exercises listed in the Tabula Rasa chapter.
3. It's not exactly individual, but maybe you can play Mockery of a Mock Interview with a friend or family member. Just ask them to role-play an interview (or meeting or whatever), and secretly decide on three distracting and/or disturbing behaviors to exhibit toward you. When you're done with the scenario, see if you can identify the behaviors and mention the conclusions you might have drawn from them. Then switch roles; playing multiple roles helps you to understand the overall picture better no matter what the exercise.

Group
(both suitable for online use)

1. **Mockery of a Mock Interview**
    A. Get a volunteer to play the interviewee and one or more volunteers to play the interviewer(s). Have the interviewee determine what position with what firm they're interviewing for. It should be something both realistic and exciting. Make sure the interviewee knows that they're supposed to take the interview seriously and try their best to get the job.
    B. Send the interviewee out of the room with a companion. In virtual environments, manually create a breakout room for the interviewee and companion. Give the interviewer(s) at least three distracting and/or disturbing behaviors to engage in during the interview.
    C. Bring the interviewee back into the room and begin the interview. Let it run for a few minutes, perhaps five. Make sure the interviewers have multiple chances to use the behaviors they've been given.
    D. End the interview when it seems to be running low on energy or coming to an impasse. Finishing on a high point with a laugh is satisfying and reminds everyone that it's just a game.
    E. Ask the interviewee what they think the suggested behaviors were, and ask them what they inferred from them. (These might be the same thing, which is worth noting.)
    F. Ask all the players about their experience in the exercise.

    G. Ask the audience what they observed.

    H. Discuss relevance. Asking people in the group to share horror stories from interviews is a good way to get the conversation started.

    I. As always, being cognizant of epistemology (how we know what we know), and the differences between reality and interpretation are essential in discussing this exercise and its meaning.

2. **Press Conference**

This exercise is based on a classic improv game or "bit" in which a straight-man expert is peppered with questions, which can be distracting, irrelevant, or inflammatory. Think along the lines of kindergarteners grilling a scientist or tabloid journalists interviewing, well, anyone. The questions should be based on willful or feigned ignorance.

    A. Ask for a volunteer to play the expert. Direct them to be as serious and authoritative as possible. They can deliver an impromptu speech on an area of actual expertise or even an existing presentation.

    B. Let the presenter speak for a while before starting the questions. Those with questions can raise their hands, interrupt, or submit via chat online.

    C. Keep pressure on the speaker with frequent questions in rapid succession from as many people as possible. Repeat questions. Be insistent.

    D. The level of outrageousness depends upon the director and the group. You can try to make it as realistic as possible, or you can turn it into an outlandish improv scene. Either way, the simulation gives the speaker the opportunity to experience pressure from an audience.

    E. Finish the exercise and process it, focusing on the speaker's experience.

    F. Repeat as desired.

19

Fake Ads

A Capstone Activity

"But wait; there's more!"—Ron Popeil

While I always set aside time for improvised scenes in full-length courses, participants in shorter programs generally don't have enough time to develop the skills needed to do these scenes. That doesn't mean they can't get a taste of performing improv though. Fake television advertisements provide a great opportunity for that. The activity draws on so many improv skills, including collaboration, creativity, communication, character portrayal, and focusing on the moment.

TV ads provide a great vehicle for this exercise for a number of reasons. Almost all of us have been exposed to them extensively, so we understand their approaches, themes, and devices. They're short, just 30–60 seconds, which means there's a limit on their complexity; character and story development are kept to a minimum. While some commercial spots and ad campaigns have been brilliant and even border on high art, most simply aren't that meaningful. That's good because it keeps the pressure low in this activity. Creating a Broadway-style musical or a Shakespearean play would be daunting, but an ad is just ... an ad. Moreover our familiarity with the form means we can easily spoof it. Indeed many current advertisements are absurd or simply low-brow spoofs of themselves.

I often end a short workshop or seminar with Fake Ads because everyone gets to (well, has to) play. Participants have a chance to work with each other and experiment with some of the topics we've addressed in the session. It's a great way to finish on an energetic, happy note. Afterward, participants are usually eager to reflect on and discuss major takeaways from the program.

I introduce the activity by explaining that I am going to divide the group into teams and will give each team an imaginary product or service for which they'll create a roughly 30-second TV-style advertisement. Each ad should contain dramatization showing life with and/or without the product or service. There also needs to be a jingle, a song extolling the virtues of the product or service. Narration may be used to help make sense of the ad.

I tell the group that each team will have some time to plan their ad and that they'll then perform it for the entire group. Everyone should be involved in the planning and creation. I solicit questions. If anyone asks how much time they have to plan, I usually respond, "some time," because I don't want the teams to dawdle. In fact, I usually give teams ten minutes, although some need more time and some need less.

I mention to the group that this exercise is a "planned improvisation." This is a seeming oxymoron that might strike some participants as almost cheating. But planned improvisation is a legitimate way of performing improv and indeed was once the norm in many comedy theaters, most notably The Second City. After performing a slate of scripted work, companies take suggestions before an intermission, and the audience returns to see what the players have cooked up. The players might have had some discussion and devised a plan but stopped short of actually writing lines. This form of improv, which was the first I learned way back in high school, is much rarer than it once was.

Regardless, creative collaboration is probably inherently improvisational anyway. You have a group of people trying to come up with something, and eventually they do. Some parts of the process are quick and magical, aha moments, and other parts can be slow and methodical. This also applies to individual creativity. What sets improv apart is that it generally doesn't allow for the refining that occurs in other creative endeavors.

Anyway, I've found teams of four to six are best for this activity. Smaller groups mean everyone can be involved, get some "star time" in performance, and share some of the pressure of developing and performing the group's ad. I create the groups by having participants count off as appropriate. So with a group of 20, we might go around the room counting off up to four to create four randomly formed groups of five (the ones all work together as do the twos, threes, and so on). Groups find some solitary space in which to work, or I send them to breakout rooms if we're online.

At this point I give each team an imaginary product or service to hawk. I try to have some ideas ready in advance so that teams don't have to wait for me to come up with something. The teams should have some wiggle room in their interpretation of what the product or service is and also how they want to present it. Sometimes I'll give a group the suggestion of a name, like "Insta-Cool," to work with and let them decide if it's a product or service and just what it does. Other times I'll be more specific; "Study While You Sleep" seems to resonate with students and "Portable Parking Space" with working people, but there are endless possibilities.

Once each team has their suggestion and starts to plan, I make myself available for questions or coaching by walking around the room, passing slowly by each group, or popping into breakout rooms online. Otherwise I stay out of the way but take note of the way the teams are working.

Some teams might finish their planning quickly and start rehearsing. If a team finishes early and doesn't know what to do next, I suggest a run-through. I don't worry about how "pure" the improv is because I'm trying to develop facility with improv skills, not to create theatrical improvisers. Other teams might need spurring. If I see a team struggling, I might tell them, "Your ad doesn't have to be perfect. It doesn't even have to be good. Most ads and jingles are terrible."

Regardless of how much time I allot for preparing the ad, I give a two-minute warning before I end the planning stage. Then I usually throw in an extra minute because I want the players to feel a little pressured but not frantic.

Now it's showtime. I ask for a team to volunteer to go first and have the other teams create an audience area and get ready to watch. If any teams are still discussing their plans, I remind them that the planning stage is done and that it's now more important to give their attention to the performers.

Before the performances I like to take a moment to remind the players of some important stage technique. For example, I remind them to speak loudly and clearly and to be aware of the "fourth wall" (where the audience sits) to ensure that they can see the audience, and thus the audience can see them. They should avoid upstaging themselves (playing away from the audience) and blocking fellow players from the audience's view. Most people will have had some exposure to stagecraft in their lives, so these are usually reminders rather than new information. Finally I encourage players to go for it, to FIZ. Commitment in performance can make a good idea great and a great idea fantastic. Likewise, lack of commitment and tentative delivery make every idea look worse.

Some days every team is excellent. Some days they're all mediocre. Usually it's a mix. I stay positive. Sometimes a team is hesitant to sing their jingle and finish their ad. They look at the audience and me for a response and I ask, "What? No jingle?!" Then the players look around at each other, and one will offer up something kind of lame and others might join in. This is great because, again, jingles almost always *are* lame, and what we're looking for in this exercise is not quality but merely *doing*. I'm the first to applaud for each ad, and I do it with spirit.

After all the groups have performed, we discuss the activity. I ask the teams how it went for them. What was challenging? What was rewarding? What did they like in other teams' performances? I tell them what I noticed and liked. There's always something to like and even to rave about.

I also ask the teams to tell us about how they worked. Most of the time I see profoundly democratic processes. Team members will stand or sit in a circle and excitedly offer ideas. There tends to be a lot of Yes-And. I often observe players emerging as team leaders while others take notes or handle other tasks. Sometimes informal subcommittees will form, with some team members focusing on the jingle while others work on the dramatization.

I rarely see one person dominating a team and can't recall ever having to intervene because of that. If they arise, domination and/or controlling behavior are worth discussing after the activity. The situation might be more complicated than that though. For example, a team might tacitly or even overtly put someone in charge because of their personality or talents. This certainly happens in the real world.

Collaboration and group dynamics are fascinating and well worth examining. There are successes, failures, challenges, and epiphanies, and, because this is a short and playful activity, it provides a good example from which participants can extrapolate to other settings and both individual and group tendencies. The goal is to have everyone in each team engaged, but if that doesn't happen, it's an organic learning moment.

If my group has the time and disposition, there's a second iteration of Fake Ads. After the teams have performed their planned improvisations and we've discussed them, I ask how they could have done better. The most common response is that more planning time would have helped. This is debatable as some pretty amazing ideas often come up pretty fast. Time certainly helps in the polishing stage; developing real-life advertising campaigns takes much longer than ten minutes.

Nevertheless, I adopt the most villainous tone I can and tell my group that, seeing as how they want more time to plan, we will do another round of Fake Ads—only this time they'll get *no* time to plan. (Cue diabolical laughter.) This absence of planning is what most people think of as improv and also makes for an extremely challenging—and potentially rewarding—activity, especially for inexperienced improvisers.

I keep the same teams from the planned ads and give them a little coaching before their spontaneous efforts.

- Keep the performing area clear. Players should stand to the side if they're not actually performing. If you're not making or responding to an offer, you're just in the way.
- Improvising well requires clarity, so being obvious and keeping one's body open to the audience and fellow players is crucial.
- Remember that you have a team to support and to support you. You don't have to have or deliver the entire idea. The exercise is like a creativity relay. Maybe you have the first five seconds, and then someone else takes over. If the team members pay attention and respond to each other, the weight of creating is carried by many hands.
- Singing a jingle as a group is easier if the players can look at the player who starts singing, read that person's lips, and sing in unison.
- When in doubt, give it the gas, not the brake. Improv is all about performing with certainty in uncertain moments. You might have a mess on your hands, but a big explosion is eminently more entertaining than a mouse fart.

Generally I ask the audience to suggest an imaginary or even a real product or service for each team just before the teams begin their performance. I'm quick to edit or alter the suggestion to make the task more palatable or easier for the performers. I definitely don't want players to struggle with humiliating suggestions.

And away we go. The quality of these ads varies, but the teams are *improvising* on the spot and doing so in a challenging format. When they're done, they're likely to look like a boatful of whitewater rafters after challenging rapids, a little shaken up but exhilarated. If the process went great, well, *great*. And if it didn't go great, the players know they survived at least.

When all the teams have performed, I ask the entire group to compare and contrast the planned improvised ads with the unplanned versions. One observation I frequently hear is that the unplanned ads are more exciting and entertaining than the planned ones. I've also heard that there's less pressure to do the activity *right* because there really is no right. In a planned presentation, one can forget what they're supposed to do and say, but that's pretty much impossible to do when no actions or speeches have been predetermined.

This gets right to the heart of improv and its value. Most of us are so worried about doing things *wrong* and not-the-way-we-planned-or-expected usually feels wrong. This feeling creates an unpleasant pressure and makes things less fun. It makes us more conservative and less bold in our performance. Freed from that pressure we can focus more on what's actually happening and the people and environments that surround us. When we're engaged in the moment and with others, something both magical and natural can happen.

My perspective as one who has performed scripted as well as improvised theater and music is that the former tends to be about doing things as perfectly as possible while the latter is more about a wonder-filled exploration.

Drawing on so many improv principles and techniques, Fake Ads are a challenging and usually gratifying way for participants to put to work everything they've studied in applied improv.

Exercises

Individual

Faux commercials are an activity designed for groups. That said, you can practice aspects of the exercise alone.

1. Think of an imaginary or real product or service and imagine its selling points. What are its benefits to the consumer? What is its appeal?
2. How might an actor portray how the product or service improves quality of life?
3. What might a narrator say about the product or service?
4. Make up a jingle, and sing it out loud.

Group
(suitable for online use)

1. Divide your group into teams of four to six players. Give them some isolated area or a breakout room in which to work.
2. Give each group a product or service and about ten minutes to plan a 30-second, television-style advertisement, complete with jingle. In online settings, groups might use special effects.
3. Have each group perform their ad.
4. Discuss the performances and the processes that led to them.
5. If you wish to move beyond the planned-improv stage, call each team back onstage individually and have them improvise a new commercial with no planning based on a suggestion you give them. A little coaching beforehand is usually very welcome and helpful. If your group lacks time or inclination for all to do a second round of Fake Ads, you can ask for a few volunteers to perform one or two.
6. Again, discuss the performances and processes. Compare and contrast the planned ads with the unplanned versions.

20

Open Improv Scenes
The Keys to the Car

"If you laugh, we're doing comedy. If you don't, we're doing drama."—Tim Johnston

Considering that my curriculum is based on improvisational theater, it only makes sense that my students perform some "open" improv scenes at some point in their applied improv experience. Open scenes are different from "game" scenes because there are no gimmicks or constructs like what you might see on, say, *Whose Line Is It Anyway?* There's nothing inherently wrong with gimmicks, and heaven knows I've done my share of them, but they do serve as kind of a safety net. If, for example, you've got a player with their head submersed in a bucket of water, waiting to be tapped out by another player, the head in the bucket of water becomes more important than anything the players say or do. Construct eclipses content.

In open scenes two players make up something together, playing out a generic suggestion from the audience or director. There's no stunt, just two players acting out a scenario. This minimalism forces players to rely on themselves and each other more than they do in game forms. There are no certain laughs created by the form itself, and there might not be laughs at all—although there usually are. Instead the players explore the suggestion and try to figure out where they're going, where they've been, and what it all means.

Open scenes are the kind of improv I like to perform, direct, and see onstage. I don't mean to denigrate any other approach, because each way of improvising has its virtues and shortcomings, but this is simply the way of improvising that speaks most strongly to me.

Performing open scenes takes time and patience and demands

that players have a foundation of improv exposure and experience. In my university courses I introduce open scenes only after several weeks of class, and I won't introduce them at all in shorter applied improv workshops unless they've been specifically requested or the group is advanced.

Getting to improvise, after weeks of studying aspects of improvisation, is exciting. It's sort of like driver's ed, where you start with lecture, reading, and watching films and progress to the simulator (do those still exist?) before finally getting to drive an actual car. You probably won't drive particularly well, but that's okay because you're still learning and you're *driving*!

While open scenes might not have the specific takeaways of the various exercises I've outlined in this book, they do draw on the same skills. Any opportunity to improvise helps develop and hone those talents. Indeed the final exam for my grad students isn't a sit-down test but rather a public performance of both open and game scenes. It's not only gratifying and fun for the students to demonstrate what they've learned, usually to their program peers, but it's also challenging and, for some, scary as hell.

Getting Started

When we start working with open scenes, I begin by explaining what they are and then ask for two volunteers. Generally speaking, scenes become exponentially more difficult with each actor you add, so two is a good place to start. I usually have two chairs in the performing area in case the players need to sit, but I instruct them that they need neither sit nor stand. Then we get a simple suggestion of a place like an art museum, or a situation like a blind date, or a relationship like a realtor and a client. Or perhaps we might start with two suggestions, like a mood and a place.

The players might have questions before they begin the scene, and I try to answer them. Most frequently I'll hear, "Do we know each other?" The orthodox approach would be that they should, but I'll usually say something like, "You can but you don't have to." I don't want the players to feel constricted by rules and "shoulds." Guidelines can be helpful, and they can also be limiting, which is actually one of the reasons why they're helpful.

I often suggest that the players give some thought to where the scene is taking place because that will help ground it and get them out of their heads. Awareness of real and imagined surroundings comes with the physical consciousness we've explored in class. Usually we'll have also worked with imaginary detail in "Space Painting," and thus the players will be familiar with the technique and value of this focus. So if, for example, the players are in a coffeeshop and they're seated, I might ask them how big their table is and what's on it. Or if they're on an airplane, I'll say that it's crowded and that they have to put their chairs right next to each other, which forces the actors and the characters to deal with their close proximity.

Then we have a scene.

Sometimes the players will create a wonderful scene. Huzzah! Usually they'll struggle, and sometimes they'll work their way through the struggles to a wonderful scene. Huzzah! Regardless, they are improvising. Huzzah!

My goal as teacher and director is to help the actors be aware of each other and what their characters are trying to say and do, what their motivations are. I try to avoid imposing my ideas on scenes but rather try to help the players discover their creative responses to what's happening in scenes. I pay attention and try to facilitate, not control. I do this by asking questions (examples are below). I might direct questions to the players so that they can articulate and build off their impulses and ideas. I might ask the audience what they think a scene is about because their perspective as viewers can help clarify things for the players who are on the spot and can be feeling pressure.

It's essential that I keep the players focused on what they're creating in a scene. Beginning improvisers (and occasionally experienced ones) are all too willing to drop everything they've created in a scene and move on to something else. Their lack of experience makes them think that important, dramatic, and funny ideas will reveal themselves in neon lights with a thunderclap if the actors can only get past the insignificant details to the big good stuff.

But really, scenes are potentially *all* good stuff, and what makes elements in scenes important is the meaning with which the players imbue them. So maybe the scene is about a white lie or a stick of gum, something seemingly unimportant. The actors must react to these things as though they are important, either in and of themselves or as symptoms of larger issues. The TV series *Seinfeld* was famously based on this premise; it was the highly entertaining "show about nothing." In life and onstage the insignificant is often the gateway to the profound.

So I stay on the lookout for players abandoning elements that have arisen in scenes. When that starts to happen, I'll say, "Pause. That [element] was important. How does your character feel about it? Play...." Usually the players will focus back on this potentially important aspect of the scene. If they don't, I'll pause them again and reiterate my direction or ask the players if they have questions. Sometimes players will create a premise that causes their character to walk out of and thus abandon the scene itself. If that happens, I pause them and ask what's going to happen to the scene and their fellow player when they leave. Then they understand that you can't just bolt.

Often improvisers will say in a scene that a character "always" says or does something or that something "always" happens. This is another way, probably sub- or un-conscious, of making what's happening less significant. If something happens all the time, why should the audience care? Part of the Passover Seder is asking the question, "How is this night different from all other nights?"[50] I feel that we should ask and be able to answer that about improvised and other theatrical scenes. So if "always" comes up in a scene, I might suggest changing it to "never" to heighten the scene's importance.

Speaking of importance, at least one of the characters in a scene must care deeply about what's transpiring. Something has to be at stake. I've discussed emotions elsewhere in this book and how important it is to have characters respond emotionally to what's happening. If both characters are indifferent, then they have no emotions and there can be no stakes. This approach *might* work in satire with experienced players, but I would suggest avoiding it. Characters must care, even if it's just one character caring that the other doesn't. If the characters don't care, why should the audience?

If a scene seems stuck, I'm likely to ask the actors how their characters feel about what's happening. I also might ask the players what their characters want from the other character or the situation. "Have your character finish this statement, with a single word if possible, 'I'm just so...' or 'I just want...'" This simple declaration helps the actors focus their attention and energy. I invite them to use this I-statement as an actual line in the scene, even multiple times, even at the exclusion of any other lines at all. This is a coaching technique I first learned from Mark Sutton as the "What's My Deal?" approach.

Actors often resist saying their I-statement aloud, even when I've specifically instructed them to do so. Perhaps they're forgetting that what's abundantly evident to them on the inside isn't necessarily evident to those on the outside. A line or action the player sees as overly obvious can be a great help for the other player and the audience. I struggled with being clear in just such fashion when I began improvising, so much so that my colleagues nicknamed me "Jude," short for "Jude the Obscure."

Clarity is essential in bringing direction out of the chaos of improv. But clarity is hard to embrace. Perhaps we're afraid we can't appear clever or original if we're obvious. Maybe we long to appear mysterious, which I suppose is understandable because mysteries are often more intriguing than bald realities. Or maybe we shun clarity simply because it seems to run counter to being diplomatic and polite, important traits offstage. Yet by being obscure and indirect, we not only miss the opportunity onstage to be clear but also offstage to be forthright, plainspoken, and transparent, among other things, qualities that are associated with honesty and high ethics.

In improv, by clearly discovering and stating their emotional agenda, players articulate meaning. This is another thing we should be mindful of in the real world. As I've mentioned previously, a little emotion goes a long way toward making things not only interesting but also understandable for your audience. By showing how you feel and that you care about your subject matter, you frame its meaning.

So, in short, finding and exploring meaning are primary goals in improv. But when you think about it, shouldn't everything have significance? If you're going to take up someone's time and energy by saying something, shouldn't it be important? If we could keep this in mind, not just in improv scenes, but in all sorts of presentations and conversations, we could have more efficient workplaces and a less boring world.

More About Coaching

- **Explore and Heighten**
  Another way to help players develop awareness and thus direction in improv scenes is to use the terms "explore" and "heighten." So a theme or behavior might arise, and you can ask the performer to explore it. For example, "Explore your

curiosity in the other character," or "Explore pouring milk into your coffee."

Heightening is about emphasizing or exaggerating a player's behavior. "Heighten rolling your eyes … your restlessness … licking your lips." Explore and heighten help focus the scene, create significance, and usually help the players get into the moment and out of their heads.

* **Silence**
Having players work in silence can be useful. Most improvisers, especially beginners, just want to talk, talk, talk. The result is scenes that are not physically grounded. When players are talking but not listening and don't seem very present, I'll direct them to stop talking. If they respond by mouthing words or using a kind of sign language, I'll point out that they're still talking, just without speaking, and that they should focus on *being* in the scene. Perhaps they can find something in the imaginary space, maybe an object, that will help ground them and the scene.

* **Trying to Be Funny**
Watch for players who try too hard to be funny. Nothing is less funny. If a player makes a joke or is forcing something ridiculous, gently call them on it. "Is that really how you'd respond to someone in that situation?" you might ask the player. This gets back to trusting process and technique. Forcing funny is like trying to force a plant to grow. You can't do it. But you can provide the plant—and the funny—everything it needs to flourish.

Of course, improv scenes don't have to be funny, although I'll admit that most performers and audiences are looking for humor from improv. One of my greatest improv moments was a scene my company did but that I wasn't even in. The overall show was comedic, but this particular scene was sweet and ultimately powerful and poignant. (I'd try to describe it, but, as is so often the case with improv, you really had to be there.) I looked out at the audience, and some of them were *crying*! I was so impressed that the players had the courage, technique, and patience to allow that moment to develop.

And funny enough, the next laugh was even more spirited because it had been set up by the scene that was so touching.

I've also seen business school students go *deeeep* in scenes and leave the audience awestruck.

Good improvisers and writers know that dramatic moments can lead to comedic moments and *vice versa* and that laughter and tears can be great neighbors. It's the emotional rollercoaster; sometimes we laugh so hard that we cry, and sometimes our crying ends with laughter. Jean-Paul Sartre said, "Comedy is pain" (only he said it in French).

Emotional grounding and having something at stake serve as solid foundations for a scene. You can build on them. The scene might become comedic at some point, but if it doesn't, you still have an interesting, good scene. The opposite of this is going for laughs too soon. If the joke doesn't work, you're stuck with nothing. Even if the joke does work, you might well be stuck with nothing. Players looking only for laughs make improv a desperate experience and rob it of its potential to evolve into just about anything.

- **Try to Make Others Look Good**
Just as improv performers are taught to make their scene partners look good, teachers and directors should strive to make players look good. One way to do that is by ending scenes sooner rather than later, looking for a high point at which to stop. If you're in charge of ending a scene, a good question to ask yourself (but not spend a lot of time trying to figure out) is, "Can this scene get any better?"

Be generous with your praise and try to stay positive. Learning to improvise is challenging and creates feelings of vulnerability. Always look for *something* in a performance you can compliment, even if it's just an impulse. Improvisers need encouragement to develop confidence, especially when they're first starting out but also throughout their careers.

Be honest and try to be accurate in your assessments and feedback. It's insulting and patronizing to say something is better than it is, and the dishonesty shows through. People know when something's a disaster, and it's okay to acknowledge that, perhaps making light of it and referring to some improv disasters of your own.

If you can be clear and honest in your coaching, you might avoid being monotonous. By that I mean that when we always use the same tone, we become less effective communicators.

You might need to shake things up so that your players still hear you. If you feel they're not hearing you, you might try being more direct, perhaps adopting a serious tone.

Don't be too rough though. I once used a little shock and awe in a theater class with a student who just wasn't getting it. I had tried encouragement, cajoling, and every other positive approach I could imagine, but he just didn't seem to hear me. Finally, late in the course when the student started making the same mistakes he always did, I shouted, "What the fuck are you doing?!" That got his attention, and he did a really good scene—but he didn't return for the final sessions, and I never saw him again. I meant well, and my approach worked in the moment, but I don't think I'd do that again.

As I look at these coaching approaches, I realize they could apply to just about any leadership role and not just those in improv. We're crossing from theatrical improv to applied improv without even trying.

Sometimes I'll offer a lot of directorial advice during scenes, especially if the players are struggling. I want the players to employ good technique because it's the best route to magic. Yet it's also important to give players lots of reps and allow them to make mistakes and work their way out of jams. Sometimes the magic happens without any intervention. No matter how it happens, I hope my players experience magic in open scenes; it really is like catching a wave on the ocean or that moment when you first balance on a bicycle.

- **Gifts and Offers**
  For improvisers, part of making other players look good onstage is by offering gifts. These gifts can be ideas, impulses, and suggestions that help the other player find their way through a scene successfully.

  Identifying the other player in some way is a traditional improv definition of an offer. "Grandma, we didn't think you'd make it for Thanksgiving dinner." "You needn't be so angry, sir, I can bring you another pair of shoes to try on." "Is that blood on your tie?"

  The Annoyance Theatre's[51] approach sees acting boldly on one's own as a gift to the other player. In other words, if your character and behavior are strong, you are by default making a gift to the other player because they must react to you and thus define their character clearly, which returns the gift by spurring your reaction.

The opposite of an improv offer or gift is asking questions. Beginning improvisers tend to ask a lot of them in scenes. Why? Because they don't know what's going on and want to find out. Questions are one way we do that in real life. However, in improv you're creating a shared reality, and your partners don't know any more about it than you do. So asking questions is just passing the creative buck. Unless it's a clearly leading question that relays a gift (e.g., "You've been seeing her again, haven't you?"), questions should be avoided.

♦ **Long Forms**

Long forms are series of improvised scenes and might be described as improvised plays. Long-form improv is a relatively new development compared to short-form (games and stand-alone scenes). Del Close is widely credited with inventing (or at least developing) this approach in the 1970s with his long form, *The Harold*.[52]

I've been performing and directing long forms since the early '90s in a wide variety of styles and structures, including musicals, multi-act pieces, genre explorations, television-style series, homages, and spoofs. There are virtually limitless ways to explore and present long forms, and improvisers everywhere are constantly inventing new ones.

I don't always have the opportunity to expose applied improv students to long form because there's already so much to do in a course. However, I believe long forms are actually easier for them than short forms. Long forms allow players to explore characters, places, and themes in greater depth than in short forms. With passage of each scene in a long form, momentum and evolution occur. Emotional high points, including laughter, tend to come more organically in long forms whereas short forms tend to create pressure on players to do something funny immediately. I've found non-theater students very receptive to long forms.

One simple long form is one you can build from the Expert Interview exercise described earlier in this book. After you've interviewed your experts and the players have had a chance to develop their expert characters, take one or more of the characters and put them in a different location, perhaps a hair salon, a restaurant, a therapy session, or a funeral. Let the experts interact with each other or other characters, and see what happens. Then follow that scene with another location. You'll find that a story starts to develop around one or maybe even all of the characters.

This is one way of approaching a character-based long form, also known in improv circles as *La Ronde*. Part of the appeal of character-based long form is that it allows players to become increasingly familiar with their characters and fully inhabit them. Intuition and response guide the player as they explore what their character wants and how it reacts to the surrounding world.

Long forms also allow more players to be involved in a piece. You might have ten or more players in a long-form as opposed to two to three in a short-form scene. All players wouldn't be involved in every scene, but each player might be in every third or fourth scene, interacting with a wide variety of fellow players and helping to shape the characters and their stories.

Other long forms focus less on recurring characters and more on themes or locations. For instance, you might suggest a theme like love, power, or dishonesty, and then have your players do a series of short scenes and vignettes that explore aspects of the theme. The scenes can last just a few seconds or several minutes, and situations and characters can return later in the piece. Or you might explore a place like a hospital, cruise ship, university, or diner, and see what happens there. Recurring characters might interact with new characters. This is a very familiar television form, although, of course, almost all TV is scripted.

One of the most theatrical and satisfying aspects of long form is its potential for exploring and creating story. A narrative arc is almost impossible to avoid. If you can imagine it, you can probably do it in long form.

While I've never had an applied improv student complain about doing open scenes, I do like to explain that the nontheatrical benefits for the participant include more experience thinking on their feet, being in the moment, and connecting with other people. It's specific practice for general use. For example, doctors with theater training show improved bedside manner[53]—a key not just to better health care but also to fewer malpractice suits.[54] That's a satisfactory indicator for me that improv is good medicine for just about anyone.

Exercises

Individual

There's really no way to improvise a solo scene. You need another person to get you out of your head. That said, if you disagree and figure out a way to do improv solo, please do so—and let me know how you do it.

Group

1. Get two players onstage and give them a suggestion (place, mood, situation, occupation, some combination thereof). If you're online, have the players leave their cameras on while everyone not in the scene turns theirs off.
2. Let them play.
3. Give the players coaching during the scene if you see they're struggling and you can help. The director's goal is to facilitate the players' bringing their impulses and ideas to life, not to impose the director's ideas for the scene.
4. Be open to the possibility that improv scenes don't need to be funny, and make sure the players are open to that too. Good improv requires patience and the courage to use solid technique. Something grounded and serious might eventually become funny, but at least it's interesting in the process. Conversely, focusing only on being funny prevents players from building the foundation of a scene. If they're lucky enough to get a laugh by going straight for a gag—and chances are good they won't get that laugh—they're going to have to follow it up with more gags because the scene hasn't been properly developed and there's nothing to explore. You can't build on a shoddy foundation.
5. Look to end the scene at a high point. If there aren't any high points, look to end it at a merciful point.
6. Discuss. Ask the players and the audience what worked and what didn't work. Ask the audience what struck them most strongly.

7. Repeat. Just like anything else, practice brings improvement. It's also true that there are such things as beginner's luck and the sophomore slump. Novices might do surprisingly well at first and then enter a sort of doldrums, which can be frustrating and demoralizing, before progressing to the next level. Dramatic improvements are often followed by plateaus. Maybe a more positive way to look at it is that the work one does during plateaus leads to periods of dramatic improvement.

8. You might find that additional players enter two-person scenes. That's okay if they're called (e.g., "Oh look, here comes Father O'Malley now"). But beware that adding a person increases the complexity of a scene exponentially, not incrementally. Still, we're just talking about improv scenes here, so how bad can it get.

9. If you have the time and desire to experiment with long forms, do! While long form can seem intimidating and is somewhat more complex than short form, it's essentially simple and organic and can be very gratifying for players, director, and audience.

10. As you process scenes, be open to the possibility that valuable nontheatrical takeaways might arise in discussion. Over the years I've found that some of the most profound and useful class lessons are not those I'd planned for or expected.

11. There are many books and courses on how to improvise onstage. I've referred to some in the endnotes and especially recommend Mick Napier in writing[55] or in person.[56]

21

Applied Improv at UNC Kenan-Flagler Business School

"This course should be required. I didn't learn any hard skills but what I did learn is much more valuable—how to overcome fear, build with others, and go for it."
—Anonymous student evaluation

Now that I've written extensively about what my course is, I'll conclude by discussing where it's been offered. The main focus of my teaching career has been in Kenan-Flagler Business School at the University of North Carolina—Chapel Hill, although I also taught in Duke University's Theatre Studies Dept. for five years and deliver shorter programs in many other academic, corporate, and organizational settings.

I hope the success I've had teaching applied improv is inspirational and encourages individuals and organizations, no matter their focus, to explore the subject. I *am* a good teacher, but applied improv is such a useful and fun study that I feel my work has been easy. I know my work has been made easier because of the great support I've received from the administration, faculty, and staff at UNC Kenan-Flagler. My gratitude is deep and abiding.

A Brief History

"Do you think you can handle MBA students?" Associate Dean James Dean asked me.

"I've worked with middle-school students so nothing scares me anymore," I replied.

With that, Applied Improvisation for Business Communication was launched as a course at UNC Kenan-Flagler in 2000. The quarter-length, for-credit offering was an elective for second-year MBA candidates. It was also, I've been told, the world's first full for-credit improv course offered at a business school. (I can't verify that but know of none that preceded it.)

After I had submitted an unsolicited course proposal to the school, my next contact came via an administrator, Jeff Reid, who had a friend taking my improv performance course at The ArtsCenter in Carrboro. The friend told Reid that he was frequently and successfully using what he learned in class in nontheatrical situations. Reid suggested I submit a proposal for a course at the school. I did and later met with Reid and Dean.

Dr. Dean, who was dean of the MBA program 1998–2002, later became dean of the business school before becoming UNC-Chapel Hill's executive vice chancellor and provost in 2013. Since 2018 Dean has served as president of the University of New Hampshire. I interviewed him in June 2016 about the beginnings of my work at UNC Kenan-Flagler.

Asked what originally interested him in applied improv, Dean said he had personal experiences improvising in business and education and saw the value of an improv course. "Sometimes there's no program or structured response.... You learn to ask questions for context and also to give yourself time to react.... You need to be thoughtful and in the moment.

"Every time I moved to a higher level, the things I do in unscripted situations became more important.... There are some things that need to be done in real time."

Dean recalled that business schools were beginning to offer some "soft skills" courses around the turn of the millennium but that they were much rarer than they are now. The quantitative nature of business study made qualitative courses seem risky, but Dean saw them as a calculated and innovative risk that stood to benefit the students and the school.

It's also possible that other factors or a combination thereof led to applied improv courses at the school. In early 2000 Bob Kulhan had started offering applied improv workshops at Duke University's Fuqua School of Business just down the road from UNC. Mary

Crossan, a professor at Ivey Business School at Western University in London, Ont., had already been exploring improv in business from an academic perspective for a decade. From my discussions about the start of improv at UNC, I've gleaned that the interest was out of the blue—but the zeitgeist can strongly influence what's in the blue.

In classic improv form, Dean saw my proposal as a timely offer. "I felt like you had thought it out," he said but also confessed, "[You didn't] really know much about business." So he gave concrete suggestions and ultimately the green light for the course.

Over 50 students showed up for 25 seats on the first day of class. Those not enrolled went straight to Dean's office after the session and petitioned for a second section of the course. Their request was granted, and since that time there have always been at least two sections offered at UNC Kenan-Flagler.

I've often wondered why there was such immediate and powerful interest in applied improv at the school. Improv wasn't as popular or widespread in 2000 as it was even five years later. Maybe it seemed novel, and students wanted a change from their usual curriculum. Maybe it seemed easier than course offerings like "Complex Deals" and "Derivatives." The school and I did no specific promotion of the course but merely offered it in the catalog.

Explaining his perspective on the value of applied improv, Michael Stepanek, Managing Director of MBA Programs and Executive Director of Academics and Operations, states:

> By establishing a new and heightened baseline and comfort with personal communication, in all its forms, our future business leaders are able to stand and deliver without the need for a projector and presentation slide deck. Beyond establishing communication skills, and enhanced confidence, students aim to overcome one of the common pitfalls of leadership—saying the wrong thing at the wrong time or failing to seize the opportunity to say the right thing when the opportunity presents itself. Applied Improvisation provides students the skills, and the boldness, to avoid the former and recognize the latter.

The course and I received immediate and consistently high evaluations from the students. Initially an adjunct instructor, I was hired in 2012 as a full-time, non-tenure-track faculty member in the school's Management and Corporate Communications area. At that point we began offering applied improv courses to undergraduate business majors (BSBA) and Master of Accounting (MAC) students in addition to the existing MBA courses. My current title is clinical assistant professor.

UNC Kenan-Flagler has offered as many as five MBA sections, five for BSBA, and two for MAC in a single academic year. Graduate sections are quarter-length while undergraduate sections last a semester. Maximum enrollment is 20–25 per section, depending upon the program. This demand necessitated the hiring of an additional adjunct instructor to teach some sections. Changes in enrollment due to various socioeconomic factors affect the numbers of sections offered, but almost all have been fully enrolled, even during the COVID pandemic. Word of mouth is excellent, and sections tend to fill quickly, with waiting lists often exceeding 50. More than 3,400 students took an applied improv course at UNC Kenan-Flagler in the years 2000–2021.

Improv has become part of the school's culture. The graduate sections present a performance as their final class project, and these events are well attended by students, alumni, friends, and family.

Time and time again my students tell me that they get to know and connect with their fellows in my classes in ways they don't in other classes. This benefits the students as well as the school. The network students create can be a huge help to them as they progress through their careers and thus increases the value of the degrees the school offers. Connections like these lead to engaged and enthusiastic alumni, which benefit schools through financial sponsorship, mentoring, and other involvement.

As Dr. Dean put it, "Building relationships and working collaboratively are the cornerstones of business success." He added that the nature of experiential learning leads to personal connections and that UNC Kenan-Flagler improv courses deepen this connection with their focus on the emotional, artistic, and "whole" selves.

Dr. Allison Schlobohm, a colleague of mine in the Management and Corporate Communication Dept., wrote the following to me at the end of a semester, having just seen my BSBA class finish their final class meeting: "[H]earing your class marching down the stairs in Kenan-Flagler belting a Blink-182 song was phenomenal. It was a part of 'All the Small Things,' and since I was a huge fan in high school, I can tell you that the specific lines were.... All of them were doing it, and they seemed incredibly happy with the experience."

Structuring an Improv Course
for Business Students

My approach to teaching business students is pretty much like my approach for teaching anyone. They're people first. I realize that might sound trite, but I come to it honestly. When I started teaching stage improv in 1990, the people I worked with came from all sorts of different backgrounds. Over time I started working with groups that were ostensibly more homogeneous, but there are always individual differences.

There are also divisions among business students that might not be obvious to an outside observer. An MBA candidate, for instance, might focus their studies on finance, real estate, sustainable enterprise, marketing, health care, or energy, to name just a few things. Some MBA students come back to school from Wall Street jobs and others from the Peace Corps or even Broadway tours. UNC Kenan-Flagler's student body has generally been about one-third international. So there are myriad and delightful differences in the MBA cohort.

In other words, there is no single business school type or focus. The one thing that we do have in common is our humanity. My job is to find intellectual and emotional commonalities and let my students draw personal and industry-specific applications. There is, frankly, no way I could ever become expert enough in their sundry specialties to tailor my teaching to them in a way that would be effective or efficient.

Our grad-school quarters at UNC Kenan-Flagler are divided into 14 80-minute class meetings, the last of which is the open public performance. Undergrad semesters have 19 75-minute class meetings. For a variety of reasons, mostly related to scheduling, I don't have BSBA students perform at course's end.

When I'm introducing the course to new students, I make a point of saying that it's experiential and that how well it goes is largely dependent on them. The more they talk and share their observations, thoughts, and feelings, the better the process will go. I have expertise I can and will share, but this is *our* learning rather than *my* teaching.

I also tell my students that I hope they have fun and that the experience will be useful for them. One without the other makes it less worthwhile. I want them to get specific takeaways—which might differ from person to person—but I also want them to gain an appreciation for and basic facility with improv. Sometimes class feels like we're in a theater department and at other times it feels like we're in a business school.

Our journey together might seem random to the participants but is one I've carefully assembled over the years and refined through observation, trial, and error.

What Students Say

In 20-plus years of teaching, I've received so much positive feedback from students in the form of evaluations, written assignments, and letters from former students that I could compile a book. Seeing as you've just read this book, I'll offer just a few examples. Naturally I'm deeply gratified by and proud of what these students have written, but, again, my goal in sharing these is to demonstrate how powerful and useful applied improv can be.

Connecting

One of my most memorable class periods came late in the semester. Jack and I volunteered.... Prior to this semester, Jack and I didn't know each other at all. But after we performed that scene together, an unstated friendship emerged. I think the act of creating connects people in a unique and special way.

◈ ◈ ◈

Never in my life have I felt more comfortable around a group of strangers in such a short amount of time. If you told me in January that I would be crawling around on the floor greeting my classmates as a sloth or crying in front of everyone while I told them about my cousin who was killed by a distracted driver, I would have called you a liar... [M]y peers became a family. We became a unit that was not afraid of being ourselves because of how accepting each and every person was. This is special.... Our classroom was a safe spot for trying new things or getting in touch with your emotions.

One of the most important lessons the people in this class taught me is to be accepting of all different types of people and to not make snap judgments. We all do this, and I may be a pretty bad culprit. When I first joined the class, I immediately tried to figure out who was who, what their "thing" was, how everyone acted, etc. I didn't at first think I would get along with everyone. I actually decided that I wouldn't like certain people in the class. A lot of my quick assumptions and judgments came from a fear that other people were thinking the same thing about me; that they wouldn't like me or had already stereotyped me into the person they thought I was…. As I got to know everyone, I learned how talented and unique each person in the class was…. Also, the people who are the most different from you may end up teaching you the most.

The FIZ

The first lesson that I've taken away from the course is the value of the so-called "F***-It-Zone." The reason that I find it so valuable is that it frames the concept of "not caring what other people think" into something less naïve and much more practical…. First, you are never going to be able to satisfy everyone, so "f*** it" if your decisions don't appeal to everyone. You certainly don't want to intentionally or avoidably affront anyone, but sometimes offending someone is unavoidable and nobody should lose sleep every single time they hurt someone's feelings…. Second, the FIZ doesn't endorse a reckless view of ignoring consequences, but rather of gathering enough information to make an informed decision and then confidently acting on that decision without regard for the sunk costs of the situation…. And finally, the FIZ reinforces the idea of being aware of yourself but not anxious…. Although the FIZ may mean different things to different people, I believe that its value consists of ensuring there is always an outlet for personality and creativity to shine through in any situation…. [E]mployees who are able to express themselves more freely create a more open atmosphere that fosters culture, motivation, and creative problem solving.

◈ ◈ ◈

I wanted to reach out and let you know that the status exercise from your class helped me land a job. I realized I accidentally packed my blue blazer instead of my suit jacket while I was leaving my hotel. After a moment of panic, I told myself there was nothing I could do. I literally said "okay, this will be a funny story if I get the job and a personal secret if I don't."

When I got to the company's office, I said to myself "don't sulk and act like you're underdressed. Keep your status level at about a 7 and hope to god no one notices that the jacket and slacks don't match."

I'm now in DC doing Business Development for Oracle. Part of our program included an initial classroom training portion, which had a pretty heavy emphasis on volunteers for examples. At the end of the training, I was given the "Trainer's Choice" award and my trainer emphasized that this was largely because of my willingness and excitement to constantly be the guinea pig in these situations.

I can confidently say that I would not have felt comfortable putting myself out there in a room full of new people were it not for your class at Kenan-Flagler. Those few weeks of training made me so grateful for the things I learned with you and the personal development I gained from business improv! Prior to that experience, I hadn't truly realized the impact your class has had on me, but now I recognize my comfort with feeling discomfort every day—and I attribute much of that to last semester.

◈ ◈ ◈

Your class of applied improv helped me handle "weird situations" better. As an example, I was standing next to my previous firm's CEO a couple of times in the elevator, just the two of us. You might well describe the situation as one with "awkward silence." I felt comfortable with it though and engaged more easily....

Yes-And

The two biggest takeaways from my Improv class have been to say, "Yes-And..." and to "be comfortable in being uncomfortable." Be it while walking up to a senior exec at my client, or a partner at my firm to introduce myself, or to take up a challenging assignment or difficult role.... As a Tech Strategy consultant, I am constantly meeting new clients and working with colleagues who bring a myriad of skills to the table. The soft skills I not only learned but also got to practice at the Improv class helped me to expand my mind to accept people who are very different from me, and patiently wait to learn the value they bring. And, of course, I will always say "yes and..." to add my own two cents.

Communication

I cannot think of a class that more directly benefited me in my current role within Human Resources at Bank of America than Applied Improv did.

I am in a lot of situations where I either have to present in front of an audience or I have to deal with an HR situation with a client within the business and I think the exercises we did in relation to thinking off the cuff and managing your anxiety/nerves to make it a positive force in your presentations is something that has proven to be extremely beneficial.

I feel much more relaxed than I used to when talking in front of a group of people and when I interviewed for this job two years ago I remember mentioning how much this class helped me grow in regard to my confidence. There are classes at KFBS that teach more technical skills that I am very thankful for but I think Improv will continue to help me with both my job and life outside of work in ways I didn't think possible.

◈ ◈ ◈

I do not have very good command of English language and also have stage fright. Still I mostly get good feedback on my presentations and training. I think your class played big role. It taught me that showing vulnerability is not weakness, it allows other persons to relate with you as human being and it makes easier to send across message. Class also made me a better listener as rather than only hearing the words, I look at the context, delivery, emotion behind the message. I know I have to still improve a lot to be better speaker, better listener, and better human being but your class provided the right direction and I think benefits are for entire life and it is for each individual to take learning to next level.

◈ ◈ ◈

I used improv extensively during pitches while founding my company to help children with autism. While I eventually merged this with a similar venture in Cleveland that was venture-backed, I went on to the role of VP of Business Development where I continued to make speeches and pitch our idea to partners, investors, and other stakeholders. My improv skills helped me prepare for this in many ways—the biggest being the realization that the audience doesn't automatically get what we feel and so we must push our emotions out to make them obvious. In a social business focused on improving the lives of children with autism, the ability to emote is a requirement for success. Your class and specifically your ability as a teacher helped me build this.

◈ ◈ ◈

Yesterday, I had my final presentation for my summer internship, which presented the perfect opportunity for me to re-apply everything that you taught me in Improv. Although I found myself getting anxious beforehand, I breathed into that feeling and focused on enjoying the experience. Afterward, my fellow interns complimented me on my composure—if only they had known all the feelings that I was sensing on the inside!

Thank you so much for helping me reach this point. The way that I carry myself is completely different as a result of your class, and I'm always finding new chances to practice my skills.

◈ ◈ ◈

I took applied improv and business to become more confident in my public speaking skills. Before this class, my preparation for any sort of presentation would start about a week before the day I was to present. During this time, I would perfect my PowerPoint slides, draft up my speech, and practice giving my speech over and over again. After all of this preparation, I would still be extremely nervous during the actual presentation. So nervous that I would "black out" during the presentation only to regain the ability to analyze my environment after I was done speaking. I was very much "ignoring the refrigerator in the road" whenever I spoke to an audience. Needless to say, I was never much of an improviser.

Yesterday, I gave my first improvised presentation. The presentation was a final assignment for business operations, and I spoke the most out of anyone in my group. Some of my group members wrote out a script as the presentation was on Zoom. I decided not to—there would be no safety net for me this time! After my presentation, I realized how much applied improv has improved my communication skills. I spoke slower and guided the audience through the presentation rather than speaking at them. I was able to "see the refrigerator" as I noticed my professor's facial expression transform into compassion during one of my speaking points. For the first time ever, I can recall what specific points I made during the presentation because I was not blind with memorization. The road to get to this point in my improvisation skills was actually kind of fun, but it was not without its challenges along the way.

Trust

Business ... is based on the interactions of and between people, so to completely overlook that primal, human component of it blows my mind. Improv, on the other hand, focuses on all things human;

how we interact with other people, how to express emotion, how to trust others....

Finally, I also learned to better trust myself. As the sad, stereo-typical lady story goes, I have a severe lack of confidence. I know that I am myself, and I know that I'm cool with that, but I feel that myself is not as smart or as capable or as prepared or as funny as just about anyone in any situation. The feeling is not debilitating, but it does kind of suck always feeling lesser. This class taught me that that's not true, not via words but through a self-fulfilling experience. I came, I tried, and I conquered my belief that I couldn't. Without going into too much detail, I walked away from several classes legitimately proud of myself, and I don't often feel that when leaving a class or a business school event. The coolest thing was that the feeling carried over into other aspects of my life. It made me feel more confident and comfortable with being myself in a number of other ways (seriously, ask my boyfriend), and to have that kind of trust for myself and who I am feels absolutely incredible.

Notes

1. Melinda Wenner, "The Serious Need for Play," *Scientific American Mind* 20, no. 1 (2009): 22–29, http://www.jstor.org/stable/24940063.

2. Thomas Gilovich, Victoria Husted Medvec and Kenneth Savitsky, "The Spotlight Effect in Social Judgment: An Egocentric Bias in Estimates of the Salience of One's Own Actions and Appearance," *Journal of Personality and Social Psychology* 78, no. 2 (February 2000): 211–222, https://psycnet.apa.org/buy/2000–13328–002.

3. Charles Duhigg, "What Google Learned from Its Quest to Build the Perfect Team," *New York Times Magazine*, February 25, 2016, https://www.nytimes.com/2016/02/28/magazine/what-google-learned-from-its-quest-to-build-the-perfect-team.html?_r=0.

4. Sam Stephenson, "The Improbable Career of John Snyder," *Sam Stephenson*, March 18, 2021, https://samstephenson.org/the-improbable-career-of-john-snyder/.

5. Michael L. Slepian and Nalini Ambady, "Fluid Movement and Creativity," *Journal of Experimental Psychology: General* 141, no. 4 (November 2012): 625–629, https://psycnet.apa.org/buy/2012–04377–001.

6. Marily Oppezzo and Daniel L. Schwartz, "Give Your Ideas Some Legs: The Positive Effect of Walking on Creative Thinking," *Journal of Experimental Psychology: Learning, Memory, and Cognition* 40, no. 4 (July 2014): 1142–1152, https://psycnet.apa.org/buy/2014–14435–001.

7. Mihály Csíkszentmihályi, *Flow:* *The Psychology of Optimal Experience,* New York: Harper and Row, 1990.

8. Marshall Hargrave, "Kaizen," *Investopedia*, February 11, 2021, https://www.investopedia.com/terms/k/kaizen.asp.

9. T.L. Chartrand and J.A. Bargh, "The chameleon effect: The perception–behavior link and social interaction," *Journal of Personality and Social Psychology* 76, no. 6 (1999): 893–910, https://doi.org/10.1037/0022–3514.76.6.893.

10. "IBM 2010 Global CEO Study: Creativity Selected as Most Crucial Factor for Future Success," IBM, May 18, 2010, https://www.ibm.com/news/ca/en/2010/05/20/v384864m81427w34.html.

11. Thomas Moore, *Care of the Soul: Guide for Cultivating Depth and Sacredness in Everyday Life*, New York: Harper-Collins, 1992.

12. Julia Cameron, *The Artist's Way*, New York: TarcherPerigee 1992.

13. Marsha Linehan, *Cognitive-Behavioral Therapy of Borderline Personality Disorder*, New York: Guilford, 1993.

14. Karyn Hall, "Radical Acceptance: Sometimes problems can't be solved," *Psychology Today*, July 8, 2012, https://www.psychologytoday.com/us/blog/pieces-mind/201207/radical-acceptance.

15. Tara Brach, *Radical Acceptance: Embracing Your Life with the Heart of a Buddha*, New York: Bantam, 2003.

16. "Personality Puzzler: Is There Any Science Behind Myers-Briggs?" *Knowledge@Wharton*, November 8, 2018, https://knowledge.wharton.upenn.edu/article/does-the-myers-briggs-test-really-work/.

17. Robert Browning, "Fra Lippo Lippi," *Men and Women*, Boston: Ticknoe & Fields, 1855.

18. Samuel Clemens, Letter to Helen Keller, March 17, 1903, https://www.afb.org/about-afb/history/helen-keller/letters/mark-twain-samuel-l-clemens/-letter-miss-keller-mark-twain-st.

19. Philip Yaffe, "The 7% rule: fact, fiction, or misunderstanding," *Ubiquity* 10 (October 2011): 1–5, https://doi.org/10.1145/2043155.2043156.

20. Y-Fen Chen, Xuan-Yi Huan, Ching-Hui Chien and Jui-Fen Cheng, "The Effectiveness of Diaphragmatic Breathing Relaxation Training for Reducing Anxiety," *Perspectives in Psychiatric Care* 52, no. 4 (October 2017): 329–336, https://doi.org/10.1111/ppc.12184.

21. "Can Standing Up Straight for a Long Period Cause Fainting?" UAMS Health, March 8, 2019, https://uamshealth.com/medical-myths/can-standing-up-straight-for-a-long-period-cause-fainting/.

22. Samuel J. Dreeben, Michelle H. Mamberg and Paul Salmon, "The MBSR Body Scan in Clinical Practice," *Mindfulness* 4 (December 2013): 394–401, https://doi.org/10.1007/s12671–013–0212-z.

23. Martin Luther King, Jr., "I Have a Dream," YouTube, filmed August 28, 1963, video, 6:46, https://www.youtube.com/watch?v=vP4iY1TtS3s.

24. Dena M. Bravata, et al., "Prevalence, Predictors, and Treatment of Impostor Syndrome: A Systematic Review," *J Gen Intern Med* 35, no. 4 (April 2020): 1252–1275, https://doi.org/10.1007/s11606–019–05364–1.

25. "What Is Method Acting?" The Lee Strasberg Theatre and Film Institute, viewed June 30, 2021, https://strasberg.edu/about/what-is-method-acting/.

26. Amy Cuddy, "Your body language may shape who you are," TEDGlobal, June 2012, video, 20:46, https://www.ted.com/talks/amy_cuddy_your_body_language_may_shape_who_you_are.

27. Marcus Credé and Leigh A. Phillips, "Revisiting the Power Pose Effect: How Robust Are the Results Reported by Carney, Cuddy, and Yap (2010) to Data Analytic Decisions?" *Social Psychological and Personality Science* 8, no. 5 (June 2017): 493–499, https://doi.org/10.1177%2F1948550617714584.

28. Amy J.C. Cuddy, S. Jack Schultz and Nathan E. Fosse, "P-Curving a More Comprehensive Body of Research on Postural Feedback Reveals Clear Evidential Value for Power-Posing Effects: Reply to Simmons and Simonsohn (2017)," *Psychological Science* 29, no. 4 (March 2018): 656–666, https://doi.org/10.1177%2F0956797617746749.

29. Andrew D. Wilson and Sabrina Golonka, "Embodied cognition is not what you think it is," *Frontiers in Psychology* 4 (February 2013), https://www.frontiersin.org/article/10.3389/fpsyg.2013.00058.

30. Samuel McNerney, "A Brief Guide to Embodied Cognition: Why You Are Not Your Brain," *Scientific American*, November 4, 2011, https://blogs.scientificamerican.com/guest-blog/a-brief-guide-to-embodied-cognition-why-you-are-not-your-brain/.

31. Guy Claxton, *Intelligence in the Flesh*, New Haven: Yale University Press, 2015.

32. Sandra Blakeslee, "Cells That Read Minds," *New York Times*, January 10, 2006, https://www.nytimes.com/2006/01/10/science/cells-that-read-minds.html.

33. "Saturday Night Fever 1977—Opening Credits—Stayin' Alive," YouTube, May 22, 2019, video clip from *Saturday Night Fever* (1977), 2:59, https://www.youtube.com/watch?v=wostlK-B9Pg.

34. "Mary Tyler Moore Show—Open/Close," YouTube, April 4, 2020, video clip from *Mary Tyler Moore Show* (1977), 1:33 (0:20), https://www.youtube.com/watch?v=9CNdgZQQkko.

35. Johannes Michalak, Katharina Rohde and Nikolaus F. Troje, "How We Walk Affects What We Remember: Gait Modifications Through Biofeedback Change Negative Affective Memory Bias," *Journal of Behavior Therapy and Experimental Psychiatry* 46 (March 2015): 121–125, https://doi.org/10.1016/j.jbtep.2014.09.004.

36. Joe Ayres and Brian L. Heuett, "An Examination of the Long-Term Effect of Performance Visualization," *Communication Research Reports* 17, no. 3 (June 2009): 229–236, https://doi.org/10.1080/08824090009388770.

37. C.L. Kleinke, T.R. Peterson and T.R. Rutledge, "Effects of self-generated facial expressions on mood," *Journal of Personality and Social Psychology* 74 no. 1 (1998): 272–279. https://psycnet.apa.org/doi/10.1037/0022–3514.74.1.272.

38. "Golden Rule," Norman Rockwell Museum, March 2018, https://www.nrm.org/2018/03/golden-rule-common-religions/.

39. Keith Johnstone, *Impro*, London: Faber and Faber, 1979.

40. Daniel Goleman, Richard Boyatzis and Annie McKee, *Primal Leadership: Unleashing the Power of Emotional Intelligence*, Boston: Harvard Business Review Press, 2001.

41. Adam Grant, *Give and Take: A Revolutionary Approach to Success*, New York: Penguin, 2013.

42. "Monty Python God," You-Tube, February 27, 2016, video clip from *Monty Python and the Holy Grail* (1975), 1:10, https://www.youtube.com/watch?v=Bj4ax1BRPqo.

43. Cary Cherniss, "The Business Case for Emotional Intelligence," Consortium for Research on Emotional Intelligence in Organizations, 1999, http://www.eiconsortium.org/reports/business_case_for_ei.html.

44. "Why Cultural Differences Are Vital for Business," University of Notre Dame, August 8, 2020, https://www.notredameonline.com/resources/intercultural-management/-why-understanding-cultural-differences-is-vital-for-businesses/.

45. Charles Green, "Why Trust Is the New Core of Leadership," *Forbes*, April 3, 2012, https://www.forbes.com/sites/trustedadvisor/2012/04/03/why-trust-is-the-new-core-of-leadership/?sh=15bdd274645a.

46. Ann-Marie Nienaber, Marcel Hofeditz and Daniel Romeike, "Vulnerability and trust in leader-follower relationships," *Personnel Review* 44, no. 4 (June 1, 2015): 567–591, https://doi.org/10.1108/PR-09–2013–0162.

47. The Sanford Meisner Center, viewed June 30, 2021, https://www.themeisnercenter.com/.

48. Will Johnson, "Full Body, Empty Mind," *The Buddhist Review Tricycle* (Fall 2007), https://tricycle.org/magazine/full-body-empty-mind/.

49. "I statement," *APA Dictionary of Psychology*, American Psychological Association, viewed June 30, 2021, https://dictionary.apa.org/i-statement.

50. "The Four Questions," ReformJudaism.org, viewed June 30, 2021, https://reformjudaism.org/jewish-holidays/passover/four-questions.

51. The Annoyance, viewed June 30, 2021, https://www.theannoyance.com/.

52. "Del Close," The Second City, viewed June 30, 2021, https://www.secondcity.com/people/other/del-close/.

53. Tom Gresham, "Theater Training Helps Doctors Enhance Patient Care with Clinical Empathy Skills," *VCU News*, Virginia Commonwealth University, August 21, 2007, https://news.vcu.edu/article/Theater_training_helps_doctors_enhance_patient_care_with_clinical.

54. Ricard P. Console, Jr., "Bad Bedside Manner or Medical Malpractice?" *The National Law Review*, March 25, 2021, https://www.natlawreview.com/article/bad-bedside-manner-or-medical-malpractice.

55. Mick Napier, *Improvise. Scene from the Inside Out*, Colorado Springs: Meriwether Publishing Ltd., 2005. Mick Napier, *Behind the Scenes*, Colorado Springs: Meriwether Publishing, Ltd., 2015.

56. Mick Napier, viewed June 30, 2021, https://www.micknapier.com/.

Recommended Reading

General

Julia Cameron, *The Artist's Way*, New York: TarcherPerigee (1992). An outstanding (if time-consuming) self-guided course on recovering and developing one's creativity.

Theresa Robbins Dudek and Caitlin McClure, editors, *Applied Improvisation: Leading, Collaborating, and Creating Beyond the Theatre*, London: Methuen Drama (2018). Not so much an applied improv how-to as a look at where and how improvisation principles and techniques are being used in nontheatrical settings.

T.J. Jagodowksi and Dave Pasquesi, *Improvisation at the Speed of Life: The TJ and Dave Book*, Chicago: Solo Roma (2015). Not all that widely known outside of Chicago and improv circles, TJ and Dave are contemporary masters of the improv stage.

Keith Johnstone, *Impro*, London: Faber and Faber (1979). An interesting and useful stepping-stone between Viola Spolin's work and that of more contemporary artists.

Kat Koppett, *Training to Imagine: Practical Improvisational Theatre Techniques for Trainers and Managers to Enhance Creativity, Teamwork, Leadership, and Learning*, Sterling, VA: Stylus Publishing, (2001). Koppett's background and bona fides are very impressive, and she's been doing the work a long time. Her book is smart and has heart.

Mick Napier, *Improvise. Scene from the Inside Out*, Colorado Springs: Meriwether Publishing Ltd. (2005). *Behind the Scenes*, Colorado Springs: Meriwether Publishing Ltd. (2015). A giant in the improv world, Mick writes about the subject as well as anyone I know. His books are interesting, useful, and fun.

Robert Poynton, *Do/Improvise: Less Push. More Pause. Better Results. A New Approach to Work (and Life)*, London: The Do Book Company (2014). Improvisational processes work in the "real" world with useful examples from corporations to science to sports.

Viola Spolin, *Improvisation for the Theater: A Handbook of Teaching and Directing Techniques*, Evanston, IL (1963). The improv bible, filled with scads of exercises and games, from a true pioneer.

Bessel van der Kolk, *The Body Keeps the Score: Brain, Mind, and Body in the Healing of Trauma*, New York: Mariner Books (2014). This psychiatrist's research into PTSD illustrates how the brain works and reveals the fascinating two-way street between body and mind. Providing a scientific underpinning for the technique I teach, this book can be very useful for all people, not just trauma survivors.

Sam Wasson, *Improv Nation: How We Made a Great American Art*, New York: Mariner (2017). The history of American improv and its role in the country's comedy.

Assigned Reading for Courses I've Taught*

Alan Alda, *If I Understood You, Would I Have This Look on My Face?: My Adventures in the Art and Science of Relating and Communicating*, New York: Random House (2017). Focusing mainly on communication rather than improv, this is an utterly delightful and worthwhile read. And, of course, I enjoy having students tell me, "You know, this Alda guy was an actor too."

Warren Bennis, *On Becoming a Leader*, New York: Basic Books (1989). Bennis' experience as a business advisor and business school faculty member made this book a good fit. A bit long in the tooth, its advice is nonetheless timeless.

Daniel Goleman, *Primal Leadership: Learning to Lead with Emotional Intelligence*, Brighton, MA: Harvard Business Review Press (1994). Extensive research backs up compelling hypotheses, although this is too dense for many readers.

Malcolm Gladwell, *Blink: The Power of Thinking Without Thinking*, New York: Back Bay (2005). First impressions can be very true or very false, and this highly engaging book explores how. The exclamation-point graphic on the back cover should really be a question mark as it raises more questions than it answers. Great fodder for class discussion.

Daniel Pink, *A Whole New Mind: Why Right-Brainers Will Rule the Future*, New York: Riverhead (2005). An intriguing look at the way our brains work and how we can make the most of them. (Some comments on Asia's role in the global economy might come across as insensitive and even offensive.)

---

* Rather than having a conventional discussion about class reading, I break my students into groups of five to seven and have them discuss it. I instruct them to share with each other what they liked and thought was useful or especially interesting about the book. Then, as a group, they should identify one to three common themes from their discussion that they can dramatize for the rest of the class. They might act out scenes from the book or come up with their own scenarios. I limit the groups to five minutes of stage time. This approach seems appropriate for an improv course, and student feedback is very positive.

Index